D1557455

THE EVANGELIZING PARISH

FRANCIS CARDINAL ARINZE

The Evangelizing Parish

IGNATIUS PRESS   SAN FRANCISCO

Unless otherwise indicated, Scripture quotations are from Revised Standard Version of the Bible—Second Catholic Edition (Ignatius Edition) copyright © 2006 National Council of the Churches of Christ in the United States of America. Used by permission. All rights reserved worldwide.

The English translation of all papal and council documents has been taken from the Vatican website.

Composite cover art:

View from church door
iStock.com/whitemay
Young Priest
iStock.com/jaroon
Rear view of a group of people
iStock.com/BraunS
People in a public space
iStock.com/gremlin

Cover design by
Enrique J. Aguilar

© 2018 by Ignatius Press, San Francisco
All rights reserved
ISBN 978-1-62164-227-5
Library of Congress Control Number 2017959086
Printed in the United States of America ∞

Contents

Introduction

Every baptized person is called to engage in witnessing to Christ according to the person's vocation and mission and opportunities in life. Such engagement in evangelization is carried out by people as individuals or, otherwise, in groups together with other Christians in some form of organized structure.

The parish has a key place among the Church structures used for evangelization as we know them in our times. It merits careful consideration.

This book is meant, first of all, for priests as a help in their work of evangelization. Most priests are engaged in parishes as parish priests or vicars or are responsible for some particular parish apostolate. A busy parish priest may sometimes have to ask himself where he should place his priorities in his work for the day. He may also reflect on how he can improve on his pastoral methods and on his cooperation with other priests, deacons, religious, and lay faithful in his parish. There are also some ecclesial movements and other associations of the lay faithful active in the parish. He knows that it is his duty to involve them in the parish apostolate. Parish priests will find this book of some help in doing so.

There may also be one or two parish priests who are tempted to think that their parish is too small or that the apostolate in the parish is not sufficiently challenging. Such a priest may not think of the many possibilities within the part of the diocese assigned to his pastoral care that have not received sufficient attention. The following reflections may help to urge him to launch out into deeper water.

There are other priests who are engaged in teaching in universities or other such institutions or who are engaged in diocesan central offices or in services of the universal Church. This book can help raise their esteem for the parish, make them ready to help parish priests when the need arises, and perhaps desire one day to be assigned to a parish.

Seminarians who are in their years of theology studies hope that the sacred priesthood is not far away. When they are ordained priests, most of them will receive parish assignments. It is very important for them and for the Church that they reflect now more and more on this basic ecclesial service that is awaiting their youthful generosity. As these future priests visit parishes and carry out assigned tasks in them during their years of seminary formation, these pages can become a useful *vademecum* for them. It is suggested that anyone who is a friend of one of these seminarians or, even more, one of their formators consider putting this book in their hands.

There may be religious Brothers and Sisters who live in the parish and who ask themselves how their congregation's charism can contribute to the parish apostolate and what they as individuals can do to be of help. Religious superiors may also need to be convinced that members of their congregation should share in the parish apostolate. This book offers them suggestions based on the theological and ecclesiological meaning of the parish.

The lay faithful as parishioners are the people who are called upon to witness to Christ at the level of the family, the place of work or recreation, in trade and commerce, in politics and government, and in other social areas of daily life. From them, people in society see what the parish is or should be. In particular, leaders of various lay apostolate organizations, associations, or ecclesial movements need a clear idea of what the Church intends to achieve through the parish and what they as leaders can do. Every layperson can say of this book: This writing is about us. It is not about "them". We are the parish. We are the people involved. The parish is our affair. It is we who should give witness to the Good News of salvation in Jesus Christ.

This book, therefore, is not an academic or canonical dissertation on the parish. Rather, it is a set of reflections and suggestions meant to be put into the hands of priests, religious, and lay faithful to help them appreciate more and more the high vocation of the parish to promote evangelization. If this writing brings improvement in the contribution of all in the parish apostolate of evangelization, then it will have been well worth the effort.

The book has seven chapters. Chapter 1 considers the parish in its position in Church life and law and then the concept of evangelization, especially with the emphasis given by Saint John Paul II to new evangelization.

The second chapter is on the parish as community. God wills to save us, not just as individuals, but also as community. Witness to Christ and response to God's call have to be at the level of both the individual and the community.

Chapter 3 focuses on the major actors in the parish apostolate. The parish priest, other priests, religious Brothers and Sisters, the lay faithful, and also their organizations, associations, and ecclesial movements are given attention.

The parish evangelizes by teaching the faith. This it does especially by means of homilies, doctrine classes, special conferences, and the spread of Catholic books. This witness is considered in the fourth chapter.

Chapter 5 is on the celebration of the faith. The parish evangelizes by celebrating the mysteries of Christ in the sacred liturgy with its summit at the Eucharistic celebration. The parish also organizes some popular devotions and other manifestations of the faith. The parish prays.

The Church of her nature is missionary. The parish should reflect this dimension. It has to move out to meet the sick and the poor, lapsed Christians, but also other Christians and believers in other religions, if there are any in the parish. This is the focus of chapter 6.

In the last and seventh chapter, there is consideration of some chosen special apostolates: the family, the young, students, the elderly, and the secular culture. Individual apostolates are not forgotten.

This book is saying to everyone in the parish: Go forth, launch out into the deep, and bring the Good News of Jesus Christ to everyone in the parish.

+ Francis Cardinal Arinze
Pentecost, 2017

I

The Parish and the
New Evangelization

In the early Church of the first four centuries, priests lived with their bishop in the same place. From there they were sent to minister to the people in the surrounding areas. They baptized, celebrated the Holy Eucharist, preached, visited the sick, and were in general at the spiritual service of the people. In feudal times, the landlords got priests to minister to their people. It was the Council of Trent (1545–1563) that decreed that parishes be established with definite geographical boundaries and that the parish priest have jurisdiction only over the faithful who lived within those boundaries. The Second Vatican Council (1962–1965) gave much attention to parishes and underlined especially the ministration of the parish priest (cf. *Christus Dominus*, 30–31).

The 1983 *Code of Canon Law* dedicated altogether thirty-seven canons (515 to 552) to the parish. It gave great attention to the question of who can be appointed as parish priest, the uprightness of character of such a pastor, his competence in doctrine, his stability in the parish, his assistants, the written document from the bishop who appointed him, and his taking possession of the parish. This code defined the parish thus: "A parish is a definite community of the Christian faithful established on a stable basis within a particular church; the pastoral care of the parish is entrusted to a pastor as its own shepherd under the authority of the diocesan bishop" (*CIC*, can. 515, §1).[1]

Normally in a diocese, a parish is territorial, that is, it is a designated territorial division along with all the people who live within its boundaries. However, personal parishes can also be created by the bishop for the people of a particular rite, nationality, or language, without reference to territory (*CIC*, can. 518).

The development of the parish follows the history of evangelization in each area of the world. In the United States of America, for example, the first parishes were marked by incoming national groups of immigrants from Ireland, Germany, Italy, Poland, France, and Spain. Now the parishes cut across such linguistic groupings. In Nigeria and many other coun-

---

[1] Quotations from canon law are from the *Code of Canon Law*, Latin-English Edition, translation prepared under the auspices of the Canon Law Society of America (Washington, D.C.: Canon Law Society of America, 1983).

tries in Africa south of the Sahara, missionaries began with mission stations that later graduated into quasi-parishes and then into canonical parishes.

Situations differ around the world as to the geographical size of parishes. In some countries, a parish might cover a rather small area. A city parish could be half a mile square, while a rural parish could vary from twenty-five to fifty square miles or more. Ideally, it would be what a priest can cover on foot. An example of this is a parish in Italy where the parish priest has lived for many years, where he knows all the parishioners by name and can visit each of them on foot. With the fall in priestly vocations in some parts of the world, however, such parishes are no longer possible in every country. There are quite a number of dioceses today where one priest can have three or more parishes assigned to his pastoral care.

A development in the opposite direction is recorded in some areas of the world. Many dioceses in Nigeria are an example. There are now many more priests to minister to the people than was the case seventy years ago. For example, what Blessed Cyprian Michael Tansi ran alone as the single parish of Dunukofia from 1940 to 1945 had by the year 2014 been divided into thirty-nine parishes with sixty-one resident priests, some of whom are indeed "in residence" but are charged, not with parish work, but with apostolates like teaching.

As a parish becomes bigger in area and/or population, parishioner satisfaction is likely to decrease, the sense of community becomes more difficult and bureaucracy more likely. The individual is more apt to get lost or to feel forgotten or even unknown. The sense of involvement can weaken. There is then the tendency to set up and encourage small basic communities where people live near one another, tend to know one another, and more readily meet to hear the word of God, to pray together, and to ask themselves how they can better witness to Christ and the Gospel. The parish is then regarded as the mother umbrella of many small faith groups. While such developments are healthy, care must be taken that these groups remain sound in doctrine, that they do not place exaggerated emphasis on their own group rules, and that they do not lose their sense of loyalty to the parish and the diocese.

The second dimension of Church life with which this book is concerned is *evangelization*. This is the sharing of faith in Christ, Lord and Savior of all mankind. Jesus charged his Church: "Go into all the world and preach the gospel to the whole creation" (Mk 16:15). "You shall be my witnesses in Jerusalem and in all Judea and Samaria and to the end of the earth" (Acts 1:8). The Church evangelizes by witness, proclamation of Christ the Savior, conversion, Baptism and other sacraments, by forming local Churches, encouraging basic ecclesial communities, incarnating the Gospel in peoples' cultures, by interreligious dialogue, and by charity works and the promotion of human development (cf. John Paul II, *Redemptoris Missio*, 41–60).

Saint John Paul II spoke of *new evangelization* in his homily in the Shrine of the Holy Cross in Mogila in Poland on June 9, 1979, and in his address to the bishops of Latin America in Port-au-Prince, Haiti, on March 9, 1983. By new evangelization, he meant evangelization that is new, not of course in its content (for "Jesus Christ is the same yesterday and today and for ever", Heb 13:8), but rather in the zeal of the evangelizer, the methods adopted, and the expression of evangelization.[2]

Applied to the parish, new or deeper evangelization makes many demands. The priest's homilies are to be well based on Holy Scripture, solid theology, and the liturgical texts. Christian doctrine is to be transmitted with fidelity, and the sacred liturgy celebrated with manifest faith. Modern communications media will have to be employed in the spread of the

---

[2] Cf. *AAS* 75 (1983): 778; *Insegnamenti di Giovanni Paolo II*, VI (1983), p. 698.

Gospel. The parish is to be missionary and outgoing in its contact with the poor and the sick, with lapsed Christians, and with the secular society in general. The rest of these reflections are going to be on what such a vibrant and lively parish should be doing.

Every parish is called to be active in evangelizing. After the General Assembly of the Synod of Bishops held in October 1990 on *The Formation of Priests in the Circumstances of the Present Day*, Saint John Paul II published his Post-Synodal Apostolic Exhortation on March 25, 1992. In this document he stressed the importance of evangelization by the parish:

> Today in particular, the pressing pastoral task of the new evangelization calls for the involvement of the entire People of God, and requires a new fervor, new methods and a new expression for the announcing and witnessing of the Gospel. This task demands priests who are deeply and fully immersed in the mystery of Christ and capable of embodying a new style of pastoral life, marked by a profound communion with the pope, the bishops and other priests, and a fruitful cooperation with the lay faithful, always respecting and fostering the different roles, charisms and ministries present within the ecclesial community. (*Pastores Dabo Vobis*, 18)

The synod of bishops held in October 2001 had as its theme *The Bishop, Servant of the Gospel of Jesus Christ for the Hope of the World*. As would be expected, it gave great emphasis to the importance of the parish. In the following Post-Synodal Apostolic Exhortation, Saint John Paul II declared that the parish is "pre-eminent among all the other communities present in his Diocese, for which the Bishop has primary responsibility: it is with the parishes above all that he must be concerned. The parish, it was frequently stated, remains the fundamental unit in the daily life of the Diocese" (*Pastores Gregis*, 45).

Every bishop undertakes a careful and systematic visit to the different parts of his diocese. The parish is the principal unit to which the diocesan bishop gives this attention. Saint Charles Borromeo was famous for his pastoral visits to parishes when he was archbishop of Milan. He esteemed such visits as the soul of his episcopal ministry. It is a golden opportunity for the bishop to meet his people at close quarters.

Saint John Paul II urges diocesan bishops to give great priority to such parish visits. He writes:

In making his Pastoral Visit to the parish, the Bishop should delegate to others the study of administrative questions and give first place to personal meetings, beginning with the parish priests and the other priests. This is the time when he is closest to his people in carrying out the ministry of the word, of sanctification and of pastoral leadership, when he most directly encounters their anxieties and cares,

their joys and their expectations, and is able to address to all an invitation to hope. Here above all the
Bishop comes into direct contact with the poor, the
elderly and the infirm. When it is carried out in this
way, the Pastoral Visit appears for what it truly is: a
sign of the presence of the Lord who visits his people in peace. (*Pastores Gregis*, 46)

This high esteem for the parish and the visit to it
by the diocesan bishop and pastor should be noted
by every bishop and should be reason for hope for
each parish priest and his co-workers.

The parish received special attention in each of the
continental synods of bishops that Saint John Paul II
held from 1991 to 1999. This dynamic pope, indeed,
organized a synod for Europe in 1991 and another
in 1999, for Africa in 1994, for America in 1997,
for Asia in 1998, and for Oceania in 1998. It is remarkable that each of these extraordinary sessions
of representatives of the world episcopate stressed
the role of the parish. Here are samples chosen from
the apostolic exhortation that the saintly pope issued after each of the assemblies. After the synod on
Africa the pope wrote: "By its nature the parish is the
ordinary place where the faithful worship and live
their Christian life" (*Ecclesia in Africa*, 100). In the
Post-Synodal Apostolic Exhortation that followed
the synod on America, he wrote: "The parish is a
privileged place where the faithful concretely expe-

rience the Church. . . . The parish needs to be constantly renewed on the basis of the principle that
'the parish must continue to be above all a Eucharistic community'" (*Ecclesia in America*, 41). After the
synod on Asia he observed: "People in Asia need to
see the clergy not just as charity workers and insti-
tutional administrators but as men whose minds and
hearts are set on the deep things of the Spirit. . . .
By their life of prayer, zealous service and exem-
plary conduct, the clergy witness powerfully to the
Gospel in the communities which they shepherd in
the name of Christ" (*Ecclesia in Asia*, 43). Following the synod for Oceania, the pope wrote: "Priests
are the Bishops' closest co-workers and greatest support in the work of evangelization, particularly in the
parish communities entrusted to their care. They offer the Sacrifice of Christ for the needs of the community, reconcile sinners to God and to the community, strengthen the sick on their pilgrimage to
eternal life, and thus enable the whole community to
bear witness to the Gospel in every moment of life
and death" (*Ecclesia in Oceania*, 19). Finally, after the
second synod for Europe, Saint John Paul II again
extolled the role of the parish: "In today's Europe
too, both in the post-Communist countries and in
the West, *the parish*, while in need of constant renewal, continues to maintain and to carry out its pe-
culiar mission, which is indispensable and of great

relevance for the pastoral care and the life of the Church. The parish is still a setting where the faithful are offered opportunities for genuine Christian living and a place for authentic human interaction and socialization" (*Ecclesia in Europa*, 15).

There is therefore no doubt that the Church sets high value on the parish. We are encouraged to take a deeper look into this ecclesial community.

～

2

Parish as Community

God is one and three. The three Persons, Father, Son, and Holy Spirit, are one God. The Father loves the Son. The Son loves the Father. The Holy Spirit is the love of the Father and the Son. The three Persons in one God are a communion that is beyond human understanding. God is love. He is Trinity.

"God created man in his own image, in the image of God he created him" (Gen 1:27). God gave man a social nature. "It is not good that the man should be alone; I will make him a helper fit for him" (Gen 2:18). We human beings need interaction with other people in order to reach the height of our potential, in order to become all that we can become.

God took note of this social nature that he gave to man in the natural order when he decided to elevate man to the order of grace through salvation in Jesus Christ. The community dimension is an important consideration in the Church. As the Second Vatican Council teaches: "God, however, does not make men holy and save them merely as individuals, without bond or link between one another. Rather it

has pleased Him to bring men together as one people, a people which acknowledges Him in truth and
serves Him in holiness" (*Lumen Gentium*, 9).

The Church is a communion. Jesus told his disciples: "I am the vine, you are the branches. He who
abides in me, and I in him, he it is that bears much
fruit, for apart from me you can do nothing" (Jn
15:5). The mystery of the Church as communion
indicates the unifying bond between the Lord Jesus
and his disciples. It is a living and life-giving communion. Its model and source is the communion of
God as Trinity, namely, the unity of the Son and the
Father in the gift of the Holy Spirit. Christians have
access to the Father through Christ in the one Spirit
(cf. Eph 2:18). The Holy Spirit dwells in the Church
and in the hearts of the faithful as in a temple and
guides the Church in prayer, fellowship, and service.
He gives the Church various gifts, both hierarchical
and charismatic, so that the Church grows, continues to be renewed, and gives witness to Christ. The
Church, in the words of Saint Cyprian, shines forth
as "a people made one with the unity of the Father,
the Son and the Holy Spirit" (*De Orat. Dom.*, 23, *PL*
4:553; quoted in *Lumen Gentium*, 4).

The Second Vatican Council, therefore, describes
this Church as communion by using figures such as
the following: sheepfold, flock, vine, spiritual building, Holy City, field, edifice, house of God, house-

hold of God in the Spirit, the new Jerusalem (cf. *Lumen Gentium*, 6).

Baptism is the door to this communion that is the Church. The Holy Eucharist is the source and summit of the whole Christian life. The Body and Blood of Christ received by the faithful at the Eucharistic Sacrifice sacramentalize this communion. Christ lives in the community of his followers (cf. *Sacrosanctum Concilium*, 7). The Church is the Mystical Body of Christ. What we do to others, especially the needy, we do to Christ (cf. Mt 25).

This concept of the Church as communion gives life and meaning to who the Church is and why and how the Church evangelizes.

The parish is the Church community at its roots. That is where most people first meet the Church. Saint John Paul II puts it this way: "The ecclesial community, while always having a universal dimension, finds its most immediate and visible expression in the *parish*. It is there that the Church is seen locally. In a certain sense it is the *Church living in the midst of the homes of her sons and daughters*" (*Christifideles Laici*, 26).

The bishop is the pastor of the whole diocese. It would be wonderful if he could meet every one of his people, talk with them, pray with them, celebrate the Eucharistic Sacrifice for them and with them, and in general witness to Christ with them. In practice, however, this is not possible. Some way has to be found to come as close as possible to this ideal. The parish is the answer. The Fathers of the Second Vatican Council stressed this point: "Because it is impossible for the bishop always and everywhere to preside over the whole flock in his Church, he cannot do other than establish lesser groupings of the faithful. Among these, parishes, set up locally under a pastor who takes the place of the bishop, are the most important: for in some manner they represent the visible Church constituted throughout the world" (*Sacrosanctum Concilium*, 42).

It is important that the parish not be seen in the first instance as the parish church or parish hall or even as the territory covered by this entity. The parish is first of all the people, the community of the followers of Christ, the worshipping assembly. "The parish is not principally a structure, a territory, or a building," says Saint John Paul II, "but rather, 'the family of God, a fellowship afire with a unifying spirit', 'a familial and welcoming home', 'the community of the faithful'. Plainly and simply, the parish is founded on a theological reality, because it is a *Eucharistic community*" (*Christifideles Laici*, 26).

It is true that the parish is not the only reality or association in which people can meet, share hopes and plans, witness to Christ and the Gospel, and live their faith in Christ generally. Professional groups like doctors, lawyers, or business people, educators, scientists, cultural agents, or even recreation clubs can be arenas for the living and spreading of the Gospel. Nevertheless, none of such cultural groupings has rendered the parish obsolete, nor does any of them entirely replace the parish. That is why Blessed Paul VI said to the Roman Clergy in 1963: "We believe simply that this old and venerable structure of the parish has an indispensable mission of great contemporary importance: to create the basic community of the Christian people; to initiate and gather the people in the accustomed expression of liturgical life; to conserve and renew the faith in the people of today; to serve as the school for teaching the salvific message of Christ; to put solidarity in practice and work the humble charity of good and brotherly works" (Paul VI: Discourse to the Roman Clergy [June 24, 1963], *AAS* 55 [1963]: 674).

Pope Francis returns to this point in his Apostolic Exhortation *Evangelii Gaudium* in 2013: "The parish is not an outdated institution; precisely because it possesses great flexibility, it can assume quite different contours depending on the openness and missionary creativity of the pastor and the community. . . . The parish is the presence of the Church in a given territory, an environment for hearing God's word, for growth in the Christian life, for dialogue, proclamation, charitable outreach, worship and celebration. In all its activities the parish encourages and trains its members to be evangelizers" (*Evangelii*

Gaudium, 28). In his address to Italian Catholic Action, at the celebration of the 150th anniversary of this lay apostolate organization on April 30, 2017, the pope comes back to the same observation and adds that the parish is the place where people feel welcomed as they are and helped to grow in human and spiritual maturity.

If a parish is to function well as a community, there are certain things that it has to strive to do. It should make an effort to "upbuild itself in love" (Eph 4:16). People in the community should seek to know one another. The concern of one should become the concern of all. The individual will then know that the others care for him. Community spirit is appreciated especially when people are in need, when they are sick, handicapped, poor, homeless, unemployed, or old. Sorrow shared is sorrow reduced. This will also happen when a parishioner suffers loss of property, is wounded in an accident, loses property by fire, or is bereaved. Concern shown by other parishioners becomes very important to the person under trial. On the other hand, joy shared is joy multiplied. On the occasion of a wedding, the Baptism of a child, a priestly ordination, a religious profession, recovery from a severe illness, or escape from a car accident, a person appreciates it if other people share his joy. A parish as a community will also find a way to celebrate a national holiday or the parish patron saint's day, a parish jubilee event, or the day on which the nation honors men or women. Religious Brothers and Sisters living in the parish will also do well to identify with the parish in its joys and sorrows, as far as their charisms and engagements will allow.

Community has to be built up. This makes demands on the parishioners. The proper functioning of the parish as community is not automatic. Community bonds have to be established, for example, by putting into writing the history and story of the parish from its beginnings, recording its key moments, challenges, and struggles, both those overcome and those still outstanding, and by helping the parishioners to know their history and show interest in it. What the parish community is and what it strives to become can be articulated. A community cannot be so perfect that it has no problems or challenges to face or conflicts to resolve. These should be honestly faced, and an effort can made to solve them. Success should be shared and celebrated. Matters still arising are not to be swept under the carpet but should be handed on to the next generation when the present people have exhausted their efforts. Every parish community is expected to think of its tomorrow, of its young people, of the next generation. The older parishioners should find a way to include the younger generation in platforms like the parish council. It is not correct to tell young people that they are the parish of tomorrow. They are also the parish of today. They are right to expect to have their share in the duties and responsibilities, in the projects and plans of the parish of today. In general, the parish community should not be hesitant to discern and discuss regularly its own health as an evangelizing Church. As many of the parishioners as is practical are to contribute in this exercise.

In many parts of the world, parishes have found that a proper functioning of small basic communities can be of help. These are small groups of people who live near one another, who meet regularly to hear the word of God, who reflect together on the practical problems and challenges of their community in the light of this word of God, and who ask themselves what concrete resolutions are expected of them. Such basic communities can also be an encouragement to the Christian family, which is called a domestic church, a place of faith, of prayer, and of loving concern for the true and enduring good of each of its members (cf. Benedict XVI, *Africae Munus*, 33). "One way of renewing parishes, especially urgent for parishes in large cities," says Saint John Paul II, "might be to consider the parish as a community of communities and movements" (*Ecclesia in America*, 41). Apart from these small basic communities, there can also be in the parish various associations for particular apostolates or to promote special devotions. Examples are the Legion of Mary, the Society of Saint Vincent de Paul, the Children of Mary, and the Societies of the Holy Name, Holy Family, Holy Face, and the Rosary, and the League of the Sacred Heart. What is important is that all such groups work in harmony within the parish apostolate. The parish priest and the parish council have an important role in promoting such harmony in order to avoid any waste of apostolic energy.

Without undervaluing the apostolate of individuals, to which attention will be given in the last chapter of this book, the parish strives to evangelize as a parish. Such channeling of apostolic efforts is not easy. It will require the engagement of one and all. People are more accustomed to asking themselves questions on how they are growing as individuals: for example, on the person's spiritual life, on how he treats other people, on the person's possible addictions or weaknesses or failures. What the parish now needs is to adopt a communal approach to such examination and discernment. What is its health condition as a parish community? What is the Holy Spirit calling this community or community of communities to do to witness to Christ and his Gospel? Is the parish hindered by individualistic or bureaucratic tendencies that in themselves may seem good or at least harmless? What new public testimonies might the Lord be calling on the parish to undertake? How can the parish council become more missionary or outgoing in living the Gospel?

In the Eucharistic celebration, the Church often

prays for unity, communion, and joint witness to Christ. In the Third Eucharistic Prayer after the Consecration, the Church prays the Eternal Father to "grant that we, who are nourished by the Body and Blood of your Son and filled with his Holy Spirit, may become one body, one spirit in Christ."

The Church is aware that she should as a united body promote peace among people. In the Eucharistic Prayer of the Second Votive Mass for Reconciliation, the Church prays the Father to endow her with the Spirit of Christ: "May he make your Church a sign of unity and an instrument of your peace among all people and may he keep us in communion with N. our Pope and N. our Bishop and all Bishops and your entire people" (*Roman Missal*).

In the Eucharistic Prayer of the Votive Mass for the Church on the Path of Unity, the Church prays God that she may be renewed by the light of the Gospel, that the bond of unity between the faithful and the pastors of the Church may be strengthened, and "that in a world torn by strife your people may shine forth as a prophetic sign of unity and concord".

The Church is very conscious of the power of the Holy Eucharist as Sacrifice and Sacrament to unite the disciples of Christ and heal divisions among them. In the Eucharistic Prayer of the first Votive Mass for Reconciliation, the Church prays to the Eternal Father: "Look kindly, most compassionate

Father, on those you unite to yourself by the Sacrifice of your Son, and grant that, by the power of the Holy Spirit, as they partake of this one Bread and one Chalice, they may be gathered into one Body in Christ, who heals every division" (*Roman Missal*).

The Church believes as she prays. The law of prayer is the law of faith. This is the sense of the old Latin adage: *Lex orandi, lex credendi* (cf. *Catechism of the Catholic Church*, 1124).[1] These liturgical samples from the solemn Eucharistic prayer of the Church show that the Church sees herself as a community that needs continued help from God in order to go on giving witness to Christ and his Gospel and promoting peace and unity among people. The parish, as a local presence of the Church, should be an evangelizing community.

~

[1] Excerpts from the *Catechism of the Catholic Church* are from the English translation, 2nd ed. (Washington, D.C.: United States Catholic Conference, 1997), of the Latin text (Vatican City: Libreria Editrice Vaticana, 1997).

3

Major Parish Actors

If a parish is to function well as an evangelizing community, the cooperation of many people is required. Among the chief actors can be named the following: the parish priest, other priests, religious Brothers and Sisters, the lay faithful, ecclesial movements, Catholic associations, and small basic communities. The contribution expected from each of these can be examined from many angles.

The *parish priest* is the leader of the evangelizing community that is the parish. As pastor, he is the representative of the diocesan bishop. The *Code of Canon Law* devotes most of the canons on the parish (canons 519 to 530) to him. The parish priest "should also be distinguished for his sound doctrine and integrity of morals and endowed with a zeal for souls and other virtues; he should also possess those qualities which are required by universal and particular law to care for the parish in question" (*CIC*, can. 521, §2). He should have a deep experience of the living Christ and be a priest with a burning missionary spirit in going in search of the lost sheep. As pastor, he is expected to be a priest with a fatherly heart especially toward the needy, the poor, the orphan, and the stranger.

The parish priest should also be an able administrator of the goods of the Church in the parish and of its finances in union with the parish financial committee. He is a key figure in the proper working out of the parish pastoral council and is the person responsible for seeing that the parish books are well kept.

It is important for the parish priest to have a proper relationship with his bishop, other priests, the religious, and the lay faithful. He sees the bishop as "the chief steward of the mysteries of God in the particular Church [or diocese] entrusted to his care; [he, the bishop] is the moderator, promoter, and guardian of the whole of its liturgical life" (*General Instruction of the Roman Missal*, 22; cf. also *Sacrosanctum Concilium*, 41). In the diocese, the bishop is "the celebrant par excellence" (Benedict XVI: *Sacramentum Caritatis*, 39). The parish priest will do well to have a clear concept of his union with the diocesan bishop and of his role as the bishop's extension and representative. His faith and devotion to diocesan unity should be evident from his words and actions. When he mentions the pope and the diocesan bishop in the Canon of the Mass, this will be a liturgical confession of this truth. Saint John Paul II reiterates this reality: "The ministry of priests is above all communion and a responsible and necessary cooperation with the bishop's ministry, in concern for the universal Church and for the individual particular churches, for whose service they form with the bishop a single presbyterate" (*Pastores Dabo Vobis*, 17).

The parish priest is to see his priest vicars and other priests in the parish as his co-workers in the Lord's vineyard. They are linked theologically by a sacramental brotherhood and ecclesiologically by their service of the parish in the diocese. "Each priest, whether diocesan or religious, is united to the other members of this presbyterate on the basis of the sacrament of holy orders and by particular bonds of apostolic charity, ministry and fraternity" (*Pastores Dabo Vobis*, 17). The Fathers of the Second Vatican Council urge religious priests to give more help to diocesan bishops in the pastoral ministry, with due consideration for the special character of each religious institute (cf. *Christus Dominus*, 33–35).

The same council urges priests to live in fraternity: "Community life for priests—especially those attached to the same parish—is highly recommended. This way of living, while it encourages apostolic action, also affords an example of charity and unity to the faithful" (*Christus Dominus*, 30). Diocesan priests in a parish should not regard community life as good just for the religious. It is good for all priests. It encourages apostolic action. It gives good example to the religious and the lay faithful. It helps each priest to grow as a human being in general human virtues. It is good for the parish that the priests at its service discuss pastoral programs and projects together among themselves. Community life saves priests from possible negative effects of loneliness and from idiosyncrasies that can creep in when a priest lives alone. It offers opportunity for jokes, relaxation, and recreation between priests. Priests should never forget the promise of the Lord Jesus: "Where two or three are gathered in my name, there am I in the midst of them" (Mt 18:20).

Many parishes have *religious Brothers or Sisters* resident within their boundaries. With due respect for the charism of each of the religious institutes to which they belong, these consecrated people can be of great help in the parish witness to Christ. As vowed religious, they show all Christ's faithful how radical the following of Christ can be. Some of these religious have in their charism the catechetical apostolate, service of the sick or the poor, education of children, the search for dechristianized people, care of orphans or refugees, or engagement in perpetual Eucharistic adoration. The parish is enriched by their presence and by their participation in its various programs.

And if there is a monastery located within the parish, the parish priest will not fail to see how spiritually elevating it is to direct his people there for spiritual retreats, advice on some spiritual matters, participation in solemn Eucharistic celebrations and singing of the Liturgy of the Hours, and a climate of silence and recollection.

The *lay faithful* are 99.9 percent of the Church worldwide. In the parish they are the largest group that contributes to the parish apostolate. It is necessary to dwell longer on their role. The priests' understanding of their role and their required theological and pastoral relationship is very important for the parish witness to Christ and the Gospel. "Because their role and task within the Church do not replace but promote the baptismal priesthood of the entire People of God, leading it to its full ecclesial realization, priests have a positive and helping relationship to the laity. Priests are there to serve the faith, hope and charity of the laity. They recognize and uphold, as brothers and friends, the dignity of the laity as children of God and help them to exercise fully their specific role in the overall context of the Church's mission" (*Pastores Dabo Vobis*, 17; cf. also *Presbyterorum Ordinis*, 9).

It is most important for the parish priest and his vicars to understand, welcome, and live this sound theology. Many problems can arise in the parish when priests do not see in the correct light their theological and ecclesiological relationship to the lay faithful and religious in the parish. The parish priest is their spiritual father in sacramental relationship. He is their link with the diocesan bishop, the vicar of Christ and pastor in the diocese. People are to see him as "a servant of Christ and steward of the mysteries of God" (see 1 Cor 4:1). He is their brother and friend in the faith. He is not necessarily holier than they are, although he should strive to be perfect as his heavenly Father is perfect (cf. Mt 5:48). He, therefore, should have this proper spirit of working with them so that the parish can be a living communion in Christ and a forceful evangelizer of the Good News.

One of the ways in which the lay faithful share in the evangelizing activity of the parish is their cooperation in inner-Church affairs. "Their activity is so necessary within the Church communities that without it the apostolate of the pastors is often unable to achieve its full effectiveness" (*Apostolicam Actuositatem*, 10). One thinks of such parish activities as faith formation programs, Bible study groups, preparation of children for the reception of the sacraments, services for the poor and needy, fundraising and building projects, and the running of the parish finance committee. In some parishes, it is not just one sheep out of a hundred that goes astray, but many more. It is absolutely necessary for the laypeople to work with their priests in going in search of parishioners who have gone adrift. Indeed, some lay apostolate organizations have specialized in effective methods of meeting Catholics who have been dechristianized or secularized.

The lay faithful also have the right to form apostolate organizations within the parish or beyond the boundaries of one parish. The *Code of Canon Law* acknowledges this right: "The Christian faithful are at liberty freely to found and to govern associations for charitable and religious purposes or for the promotion of the Christian vocation in the world; they are free to hold meetings to pursue these purposes in common" (*CIC*, can. 215). "Maintaining the proper relationship to Church authorities, the laity have the right to found and control such associations and to join those already existing", says the Second Vatican Council in *Apostolicam Actuositatem*, 19 (cf. also *Lumen Gentium*, 37). Saint John Paul II lists five criteria that are needed to guarantee the proper ecclesial nature and acceptance of such lay associations: primacy is to be given to the call of every Christian to holiness; the Catholic faith is to be professed; there should be strong and authentic communion with the pope and the bishop; there should be conformity to and participation in the Church's apostolic goals;

and, in view of the Church's social doctrine, there should be a commitment to a presence in human society that places the organization at the service of the dignity of the person (cf. *Christifideles Laici*, 30). If these conditions are observed, no cleric need be afraid of the lay apostolate. Indeed, the freedom and right of the lay faithful to form such apostolate organizations are not a concession by priests or bishops, for they flow from the Sacrament of Baptism, which calls on all the baptized to communion and mission.

The apostolate of the lay faithful goes beyond their cooperation with the clerics in inner-Church affairs. Indeed, the specific apostolate of the laity is the evangelization of the secular order. The laity are called to bring the spirit of Christ into the family, the place of work and recreation, the various professions, politics and government, national and international affairs. The Second Vatican Council is very clear on this:

> Laymen should also know that it is generally the function of their well-formed Christian conscience to see that the divine law is inscribed in the life of the earthly city; from priests they may look for spiritual light and nourishment. Let the layman not imagine that his pastors are always such experts, that to every problem which arises, however complicated, they can readily give him a concrete solu-

tion, or even that such is their mission. Rather, en-lightened by Christian wisdom and giving close at-tention to the teaching authority of the Church, let the layman take on his own distinctive role. (*Gau-dium et Spes*, 43)

The council teaches this same doctrine in its docu-ment on the Church (*Lumen Gentium*, 30–38) and in its decree on the lay apostolate (*Apostolicam Actuosi-tatem*, 2, 7). It is important for the Church that every priest shares these convictions. This will mean that the priest not only leaves the lay faithful full free-dom to carry out this specific apostolate, but also supports them in it. The engagement of the laity in this evangelization of the temporal order will of-ten go beyond parish boundaries and require action from the diocesan bishop. Such would be the case, for example, with reference to the appointment of a priest chaplain for people in political action or for Catholic medical workers, lawyers or teachers, or for scientists and people who work in the public sphere, for the defense of marriage and the family and the respect due to some cultural values. It would be ex-cellent if every diocesan bishop looked into this.

Among the actors in the parish that evangelizes are *small Christian communities*, which in some countries are called basic ecclesial communities. As already re-called above, they are associations of people who live near one another, who meet regularly to share the word of God, and who in this light ask themselves what the Lord expects of them in their concrete, everyday life. It is important that such groups work in close cooperation with the parish priest and with parish programs.

Deserving of longer treatment are *ecclesial movements or associations*. In the universal Church, they have flourished particularly in the past half century since the Second Vatican Council. They generally hold a weekly or other regular meeting for their members. They offer opportunity for catechesis, for the spiritual nourishment of their members, for initiation into the Bible and prayer and for the development of friendships among fellow Catholics. Members are helped to apply Church teachings to family, society, work, and service of the poor. These movements have demonstrated an admirable capacity to evangelize. Recent popes like Saint John Paul II and Benedict XVI have given them great support as gifts of the Holy Spirit to the Church of our time.

With differing emphasis, these movements make room for professionals to join and be enriched. Many of them have given rise to priestly or religious vocations. They are not afraid to go to the people on the existential peripheries of life, like people in slums, lapsed Catholics, or nonbelievers. Some specialize in peace promotion, in ecumenical activities, in interreligious relations, or simply in looking after the homeless and the hungry. As a parish gets bigger and bigger and tends to become more bureaucratic, the energy and enthusiasm brought by such communities become even more needed.

Examples of such ecclesial movements or associations are the Focolare Movement, the Neocatechumenal Way, Opus Dei, Communion and Liberation, the Community of the Beatitudes, and the Community of Sant'Egidio. By this listing, there is no desire to suggest that they are all following a straitjacket paradigm. Each of them is different and has its own charism. One common trait is the fact that the Holy Spirit seems to be saying something to the Church through each of them. They have a type of evangelical freshness. They motivate Catholics who want to do something more for the spread of the Gospel. They help to reduce the danger of anonymity in the parish. They are missionary and outgoing. And they often reach where priests and bishops may not easily do so.

In order for these potentials to be realized, it is useful to beware of the possible tendency of such movements to divide parishes into "real Catholics" and "others" or to assume, almost unknowingly, a superiority complex that will eventually alienate the other parishioners. If they appear to be developing a

parallel parish, it is understandable if the parish priest
and the bishop become apprehensive. This is another
way of saying that there should be good understanding between the leaders of these movements and the
priests and the bishop. Occasionally, a parish priest
may feel that one or two movements have pulled
out his best parishioners from active participation in
direct parish programs. Since most of these associations or movements go beyond the parish in their
organization and functioning, the bishop of the diocese and his assistants have obvious responsibilities
in the matter. And all clerics should do their best
to be well informed on the charisms of these movements, since this will greatly help in achieving the
required cooperation, aimed at the full evangelizing
activity of the Church on both parish and diocesan
levels.

Formation and training in leadership skills are needed
by both the lay faithful and the religious Brothers
and Sisters who work with the priests in the parish
apostolate. The *Code of Canon Law* appreciates this
need: "Lay persons who devote themselves permanently or temporarily to some special service of the
Church are obliged to acquire the appropriate formation which is required to fulfill their function properly and to carry it out conscientiously, zealously,
and diligently" (*CIC*, can. 231, §1). The exercise

of leadership requires training. Encouragement, opportunity, and special courses, which must include sound theology and sociology, are needed if energy is not to be wasted in a power struggle within the parish.

Religious Brothers and Sisters and lay organizations that work in the parish will not lack some members who can fulfill leadership roles better than others. Such potential leaders need to be identified, given proper coaching, and encouraged to exercise their gifts. The parish priest should spend more time with such leaders than with the general body of religious or lay faithful. Such leaders will thus gradually share a clearer understanding of parish projects, the means to achieve them, and practical knowledge on how to proceed. An able parish priest has nothing to fear from well-prepared leaders from among the lay faithful or the religious.

Detachment to a certain extent is required of every parish worker. No doubt, fidelity to and love for the parish apostolate should mark each of these actors who have been considered: priests, religious Brothers and Sisters, lay faithful, or members of ecclesial movements or of Catholic associations. With all of them, the best expression of the Christian spirit is to love the parish, to be faithful to its apostolate, to be ready to make big sacrifices to see the parish become an actively evangelizing one, and to rejoice at its apostolic successes and be sad at its failures or reverses.

Nevertheless, one should also mention the temptation to be overly attached to a particular parish. It is possible for a worker in a parish to end up thinking that without him the parish would not succeed or would lose much of its evangelizing vitality. Such a temptation is not beyond the realm of possibility. Reflection and discernment may be needed to detect it. One proof of someone trapped by such a temptation can be seen, for example, in the case of a parish priest when a transfer to another parish is proposed or decided by the bishop. The overly attached priest can begin to marshal all kinds of arguments against the proposed transfer.

Here is a story that illustrates the point being made. Parishioners who became overly attached to one priest organized a large number of people from the parish to go to the bishop and argue that if their parish priest were transferred, the parish would lose its main driving force and that, moreover, the priest was doing very well and so should not be sent away. The bishop replied that if indeed the parish would collapse at the transfer of that priest, then that would be an argument in favor of his immediate transfer, because it would mean that he had not encouraged and involved enough parishioners as leaders but had made himself indispensable or had been running a "one-man show". And when the people responded that the priest was doing very well, the bishop suggested that in that case it would be a good idea to transfer him to another parish, so that he could perform similar good work there, since the present parish should not try to monopolize the services of such an able priest. The bishop, moreover, promised them that the new parish priest whom he intended to send them would also be a Catholic priest!

The reader can see from all this that what is required of all actors in the parish, be they priests, religious, or lay faithful, is indeed faithful service and love of the parish, but without undue attachment to people or places. This is easy to say but difficult to carry out. And yet it is necessary for all followers of Christ to strive to develop and live this spirit. Only Christ is indispensable in his Church. His followers do not forget that he said to them: "When you have done all that is commanded you, say, 'We are unworthy servants; we have only done what was our duty'" (Lk 17:10). It is interesting that Saint Benedict, in chapter 57 of the *Rule of Saint Benedict*, gives the direction that if the abbot sees that a monk craftsman is taking undue pride in his work, the abbot should reassign him.

4

The Parish Teaching the Faith

The parish that evangelizes cannot undervalue the teaching of the Catholic faith. The Second Vatican Council goes to great lengths to spell out the teaching role of priests and bishops: "In exercising this care of souls, pastors and their assistants should so fulfill their duty of teaching, sanctifying and governing that the faithful and the parish communities will truly realize that they are members both of the diocese and of the universal Church" (*Christus Dominus*, 30). The council spells out in greater detail what it means by the teaching office:

> In the exercise of their teaching office it is the duty of pastors to preach God's word to all the Christian people so that, rooted in faith, hope and charity, they will grow in Christ, and as a Christian community bear witness to that charity which the Lord commended. It is also the duty of pastors to bring the faithful to a full knowledge of the mystery of salvation through a catechetical instruction which is consonant with each one's age. In imparting this instruction they should seek not only the assistance of religious but also the cooperation of the laity,

establishing also the Confraternity of Christian Doctrine. (*Christus Dominus*, 30)

Sacred Scripture has a key and honored place in the imparting of Christian doctrine. The *General Directory for Catechesis* in 1997 insisted: "Sacred Scripture as 'the word of God written under the inspiration of the Holy Spirit', and the *Catechism of the Catholic Church*, as a significant contemporary expression of the living Tradition of the Church and a sure norm for teaching the faith, are called, each in its own way and according to its specific authority, to nourish catechesis in the Church of today" (Congregation for the Clergy on August 15, 1997, *General Directory for Catechesis*, 128). A world synod of bishops was celebrated in 2008 on *The Word of God in the Life and Mission of the Church*. The synod called for a particular pastoral commitment to appreciating the centrality of the word of God in the Church's life. The Bible is to inspire all pastoral work. Pope Benedict XVI explains: "This does not mean adding a meeting here or there in parishes or dioceses, but rather examining the ordinary activities of Christian communities, in parishes, associations and movements, to see if they are truly concerned with fostering a personal encounter with Christ, who gives himself to us in his word" (*Verbum Domini*, 73). Every parish should encourage its people to have the Bible enthroned in a prominent place in their home. Families will do well to arrange a common reading of the Sacred Scripture each day, or at least on Sundays. Small groups of parishioners who read the Bible together and strive to pray with the sacred text as an inspiration are to be encouraged. It will be useful for the parish priest or one of his assistant priests to meet with the leaders of such groups occasionally to make sure that the Bible groups do not begin to introduce unorthodox understandings of the sacred text.

People will gradually learn by frequent reading of the Bible "the surpassing worth of knowing Christ Jesus" (Phil 3:8). The parish priest will not forget the important observation of Saint Jerome that "ignorance of the Scriptures is ignorance of Christ" (*Commentary on Isaiah, Prol.: PL* 24:17, as quoted in *Dei Verbum*, 25). Due attention to the Bible will also be a good answer to the proliferation of sects that tend to distort or to manipulate the reading of Sacred Scripture. Priests should be well prepared, right from their years in the seminary, to help the lay faithful to know the Bible, to procure a personal copy, to read it for at least fifteen minutes a day, and to allow themselves to be nourished by it.

The *Catechism of the Catholic Church* has an honored place as a text in the teaching office of the Church in our times. After excellent preparation, it was officially published and given to the Church by Saint John Paul II by his Apostolic Constitution *Fidei Depositum* (October 11, 1992), on the thirtieth anniversary of the opening of the Second Vatican Council. The saintly pope declared it "a statement of the Church's faith and of Catholic doctrine, attested to or illumined by Sacred Scripture, the Apostolic Tradition and the Church's Magisterium". He also declared it to be "a valid and legitimate instrument for ecclesial communion and a sure norm for teaching the faith" (*Fidei Depositum*, IV). This great document is "a full, complete exposition of Catholic doctrine, enabling everyone to know what the Church professes, celebrates, lives, and prays in her daily life. . . . Catechesis will find in this genuine, systematic presentation of the faith and of Catholic doctrine a totally reliable way to present, with renewed fervor, each and every part of the Christian message to the people of our time." So Saint John Paul II wrote in his Apostolic Letter *Laetamur Magnopere* (August 15, 1997), on the occasion of the approval and promulgation of the Latin typical edition of the Catechism.

Every parish priest should treasure this Catechism as a major teaching document. He will find that this masterly text faithfully and systematically presents the teaching of Holy Scripture, the living Tradition of the Church, and the teaching of the Magisterium. At the same time, the Catechism includes a rich spiritual heritage from the Fathers of the Church and from her Doctors and saints. Every priest will find in this book solid material for most of his homilies and for special talks on the various articles of the Catholic faith. Diocesan officials who look after the religious education of children in school and out of school will find in the *Catechism of the Catholic Church* abundant help for the inspiration and eventual production of shorter catechetical texts for groups of the faithful. Bishops and their assistants will also find this Catechism an important guide in giving their approval of local catechetical and other faith-teaching publications.

This Catechism goes a long way to help priests and bishops meet their responsibility to see that the lay faithful get adequate religious instruction. The *Code of Canon Law* insists that "lay persons are bound by the obligation and possess the right to acquire a knowledge of Christian doctrine adapted to their capacity and condition so that they can live in accord with that doctrine, announce it, defend it when necessary, and be enabled to assume their role in exercising the apostolate" (*CIC*, can. 229, §1).

A word must be said here about the old habit of getting children to commit catechetical formulae to memory. Priests and catechists should note that memorization is not old-fashioned. Pope Benedict appreciates and praises "judicious *memorization* of some passages which are particularly expressive of the Christian mysteries" (*Verbum Domini*, 74). While knowledge of the faith does not depend primarily on memorization of texts, nevertheless it would be a mistake to overlook the usefulness for children in being able to express the main tenets of the faith by memory. The question-and-answer system of the older catechisms should not be regarded as overtaken by modern progress in catechetics. It is notable that the *Compendium of the Catechism of the Catholic Church*, approved and published by Pope Benedict XVI on June 28, 2005, has 598 questions and answers.[1] The Baltimore Catechism of old and the earlier Igbo Catechism in Nigeria contain excellent summaries of the faith. It is most helpful for Christians to memorize these model texts in their youth, because as they grow older, they will gradually understand better what those statements mean. I have noticed that when I quote such Catechism summaries in homilies and add a scriptural and dogmatic commentary, people, beginning with the older ones, nod their heads in approval. If the person who conducts a catechism

---

[1] *Compendium, Catechism of the Catholic Church* (Libreria Editrice Vaticana; Washington, D.C.: United States Conference of Catholic Bishops, 2006).

class today is well instructed in theology and Scripture, such a teacher will be able with adequate commentaries to present these texts to be memorized. The *Catechism of the Catholic Church* offers the teacher of the faith abundant and rich texts from Holy Scripture, the Tradition of the Church, the Magisterium, and writings from Church Fathers and saints. From such sources, questions and answers can be enriched and memorization will be found to serve a very useful purpose.

The provision of adequate books on the faith for the people is part of the teaching responsibility of priests and bishops. The Bible is the first book that should be in the hands of every Catholic who can read. Pope Francis in his Angelus Message of March 5, 2017, advised that as most people now have a cell phone in their pockets, so they should also have a pocket edition of the Bible with them wherever they go. Bishops' conferences have the duty and authority to approve Bible translations. The parish priest will find the Bible edition most suitable for his people. In our times, some cell phones, iPads, and computers have applications that provide good editions of the Bible in various languages. Missals are the next book to be recommended for all parishioners so that they will be able to prepare the Mass texts even before they come to church, to follow the sacred rite of the

Eucharistic celebration, and to pray with the texts afterward. There are documents from the pope and others from the bishop that the people should read. Books on the Catholic faith written by approved theologians, Catholic periodicals, and diocesan and parish bulletins are not lacking. The various modern media also bring the faith to the knowledge of the public in CDs and DVDs of many types. It will be found helpful for the parish priest to keep his people well informed on these documents. Where a parish Catholic bookshop is not feasible, at least there will be a diocesan bookshop where all such publications can be found. In our times when we lament the fact that there are many publications that do damage to marriages and the family, that propagate pornography or attack the Catholic faith, that give the people wrong interpretations of the Bible, or that extol sects or fake apparitions, it is ever more important and useful to put positive and faith-nourishing publications into people's hands. The best answer to darkness is light, not a lecture on the negative effects of darkness.

The tradition of *organizing children in different classes* for preparation for the reception of the sacraments should be maintained in parishes. Children already baptized in infancy need to be prepared for the reception of the Sacraments of Penance, Holy Eucharist, and Confirmation. While religious education in Catholic schools can already achieve much, the parish should make provision for special catechism classes for the reception of these sacraments. It may not be ideal for all the children in a school class to be promoted at the same time to these sacraments. Some of them may actually not be sufficiently instructed. In some cases, there may not have been enough contact between the parish priest and the parents of the child. Since it will not be easy to persuade young people and adults to continue to come to catechism classes after they are confirmed, the children who are not sufficiently instructed at the time of the reception of these sacraments are likely to suffer the effects of this neglect and their consequent ignorance for the rest of their lives. Let it also be added that adults who are to receive Baptism or converts into the Catholic faith from other Christian communities need special classes. This is rather demanding on the parish priest and his assistants. But it is necessary. Here, faithful adherence to the process of *The Christian Initiation of Adults* (RCIA) comes in. Religious ignorance cannot be anything but an obstacle in the living of the faith.

The homily is a major area of responsibility for the parish priest. Particularly in the Eucharistic celebration, he delivers a homily to his people. Shorter

homilies also have place in other liturgical celebrations. The homily should be a beautiful presentation
based on the liturgical texts, on Holy Scripture, and
on sound theology. "Preaching", says Pope Francis, "should guide the assembly, and the preacher, to
a life-changing communion with Christ in the Eucharist. This means that the words of the preacher
must be measured, so that the Lord, more than his
minister, will be the center of attention" (*Evangelii
Gaudium*, 138). Pope Benedict XVI urges ministers
to "preach in such a way that the homily closely re-
lates the proclamation of the word of God to the
sacramental celebration and the life of the community, so that the word of God truly becomes the
Church's vital nourishment and support" (*Sacramentum Caritatis*, 46). "The preacher has the wonderful
but difficult task of joining loving hearts, the hearts
of the Lord and his people" (*Evangelii Gaudium*, 143).

It is desirable for the homily to strive to cover
most areas of the Catholic faith over a period of
about three years. The priest must not allow himself
to be influenced by the temptation to speak to his
people only on what they like to hear and to avoid
unpopular topics like Christian demands on justice
and chastity. The synod of bishops held in 2005 requests priests not to avoid preaching on such topics. Pope Benedict summarizes this concern: "During the course of the liturgical year it is appropriate

to offer the faithful, prudently and on the basis of the three-year lectionary, 'thematic' homilies treating the great themes of the Christian faith, on the basis of what has been authoritatively proposed by the Magisterium in the four 'pillars' of the *Catechism of the Catholic Church*, and the recent *Compendium*, namely: the profession of faith, the celebration of the Christian mystery, life in Christ and Christian prayer" (*Sacramentum Caritatis*, 46).

The homily should not be too long. There is a limit to what the people can absorb in one sitting. It should not become a lecture on biblical exegesis or a parade of theological acrobatics. Much less should the homily degenerate into a campaign for money for Church projects or, worse still, into sociological analysis or a commentary on current political activities. Obviously the homily is not the opportunity to rebuke those parishioners who do not come to Mass! "The homily", notes Pope Francis, "is the touchstone for judging a pastor's closeness and ability to communicate to his people" (*Evangelii Gaudium*, 135). A good homily demands careful and prayerful preparation from the priest. Pope Francis clearly rebukes the priest who is negligent on this point: "A preacher who does not prepare is not 'spiritual'; he is dishonest and irresponsible with the gifts he has received" (*Evangelii Gaudium*, 145).

On June 29, 2014, the Congregation for Divine

Worship and the Discipline of the Sacraments issued a beautiful thirty-six-paragraph Directory on
Homiletics (in *Notitiae*, January to June 2015, pp.
65–88). This document offers a preacher all the advice he needs in order to deliver the word of God
with due respect and the hoped-for effectiveness.

Catechists offer an important service in the parish.
They teach the faith. They initiate beginners into the
life of the Church community. They prepare groups
of the faithful for the reception of the various sacraments. They lead the local Catholic community in
prayer in the absence of the priest. And they assist the
parish priests in other ways. The *Code of Canon Law*
stresses the importance of their role: "Catechists are
to be employed in carrying out missionary work; catechists are those lay members of the Christian faithful who have been duly instructed, who stand out
by reason of their Christian manner of life, and who
devote themselves to expounding the gospel teaching and organizing liturgical functions and works of
charity" (*CIC*, can. 785, §1).

It will be appreciated that catechists are needed,
not only in countries of recent evangelization, but
also where the Church has been established for centuries. It is inspiring that the Diocese of Rome has
quite a number of catechists. It goes without saying
that proper formation is needed for catechists both

initially and in an on-going fashion (cf. *CIC*, can. 785, §2). Where they are full-time parish workers, it is expected that they will receive adequate remuneration.

Special lectures for a deepening in the faith can be organized in some parishes. At times, it will be found more suitable for several neighboring parishes to join hands to arrange one conference. The Sunday homily is not enough for all parishioners. There are people who, because of their level of general culture or because of their profession (like medical workers, legal practitioners, politicians, educators, or business people), need to go deeper in their knowledge of the faith and its demands on life in the world of today. Specialists on various scriptural, theological, or pastoral questions can be invited to lead people in a deeper reflection on the faith. Such conferences will make room for questions and answers, which is a possibility that the homily cannot offer. A lecture provides an opportunity to introduce to the people books like the *Catechism of the Catholic Church*, its *Compendium*, and the 525-page *Compendium of the Social Doctrine of the Church*.[2]

[2] Pontifical Council for Justice and Peace, *Compendium of the Social Doctrine of the Church* (Libreria Editrice Vaticana; Washington, D.C.: United States Conference of Catholic Bishops, 2004).

Blessed is the parish that sees its pastor exercising faithfully his teaching office. Such a parish will thus be better motivated and energized to evangelize.

~

5

The Evangelizing Parish Prays

Prayer is a necessary part of the evangelizing activity of the Church. Effective witness to Christ is not an exercise to be achieved by mere human effort. Jesus has taught us about our dependence on him: "As the branch cannot bear fruit by itself, unless it abides in the vine, neither can you, unless you abide in me. I am the vine, you are the branches. He who abides in me, and I in him, he it is that bears much fruit, for apart from me you can do nothing" (Jn 15:4–5). The teaching of the Lord Jesus could not be clearer.

The Church has striven to live this teaching and has understood the importance of prayer for all who want to evangelize, both individuals and communities. After the Ascension of Christ, the eleven Apostles "with one accord devoted themselves to prayer, together with the women and Mary the mother of Jesus, and with his brethren" (Acts 1:14). After the coming of the Holy Spirit on Pentecost day, the preaching by Saint Peter and the conversion of three thousand people, this early Christian community "held steadfastly to the apostles' teaching and fellowship, to the breaking of the bread and to the prayers" (Acts 2:42). "This sequence", says the *Catechism of the Catholic Church*, "is characteristic of the Church's prayer: founded on the apostolic faith; authenticated by charity; nourished in the Eucharist" (2624).

Prayer is a vital necessity both in the spiritual life of each Christian and in the apostolic engagement of the individual and of the Church community. Saint Alphonsus Liguori uses rather strong language: "Those who pray are certainly saved; those who do not pray are certainly damned" (*Del Gran Mezzo della Preghiera*, as quoted in *CCC* 2744). The *Catechism of the Catholic Church* insists: "Prayer and *Christian life* are *inseparable*, for they concern the same love and the same renunciation, proceeding from love; the same filial and loving conformity with the Father's plan of love; the same transforming union in the Holy Spirit who conforms us more and more to Christ Jesus; the same love for all men, the love with which Jesus has loved us. 'Whatever you ask the Father in my name, he [will] give it to you' [Jn 15:16]" (*Catechism of the Catholic Church*, 2745). The great Christian writer Origen puts the necessary connection between prayer and active apostolic works this way: "He 'prays without ceasing' who unites prayer to works and good works to prayer. Only in this way can we consider as realizable the principle of praying without ceasing" (*De Orat.* 12, *PG* 11:452C, as quoted in *CCC* 2745).

The prayer life of the evangelizing parish can be discussed under the following headings: the Holy Eucharist and the other sacraments; the Liturgy of the Hours; Marian devotion; other non-liturgical community prayers, and personal prayer.

The Holy Eucharist and its various forms of celebration occupy a central place in the liturgical life of the Church. The public worship the Church, or the sacred liturgy, "is the summit toward which the activity of the Church is directed; at the same time it is the font from which all her power flows" (*Sacrosanctum Concilium*, 10). Within the sacred liturgy, the Eucharist has the highest and central position. The Eucharistic Sacrifice is described by the Second Vatican Council as "the fount and apex of the whole Christian life" (*Lumen Gentium*, 11). The council continues to stress the central role that the Holy Eucharist has in the prayer life and apostolate of the Church: "The renewal in the Eucharist of the covenant between the Lord and man draws the faithful into the compelling love of Christ and sets them on fire. From the liturgy, therefore, and especially from the Eucharist, as from a font, grace is poured forth upon us; and the sanctification of men in Christ and the glorification of God, to which all other activities of the Church are directed as toward their end, is achieved in the most efficacious possible way" (*Sacrosanctum Concilium*, 10). The parish must therefore pay great attention to the celebration of the Eucharistic Sacrifice and to the worship of our Lord in this great Sacrament outside Mass.

The first thing that the parish priest has to do is to look into his faith in this mystery of faith that is the Holy Eucharist. Both his doctrinal preparation and, even more, his manifestation of this faith in all his dealings with this inestimable gift of Christ to his Bride the Church have much influence on the parish community. The way in which the priest celebrates Mass becomes, in a sense, a homily without words because it manifests his faith. If he has great reverence for Jesus in this sacrifice and sacrament, and if he respects the liturgical laws and directives of the Church in all that touches his Eucharistic ministration, such an approach of faith will be shown to the people in a convincing way. The priest never forgets the truth contained in the dictum *lex orandi, lex credendi* (or *legem credendi lex statuat supplicandi*), credited to Prosper of Aquitaine: the law of prayer is the law of faith: the Church believes as she prays (cf. *Catechism of the Catholic Church*, 1124). The priest's manner of celebrating the Holy Eucharist manifests his faith and influences the congregation.

It is therefore no surprise that the *Code of Canon Law* insists that "the pastor is to see to it that the Most Holy Eucharist is the center of the parish assembly of the faithful; he is to work to see to it that the Christian faithful are nourished through a devout celebration of the sacraments and especially that they frequently approach the sacrament of the Most Holy Eucharist and the sacrament of penance. . . . The pastor must supervise [the sacred liturgy] in his parish under the authority of the diocesan bishop, being vigilant lest any abuses creep in" (*CIC*, can. 528, §2).

While the parish priest is to see that Holy Mass is celebrated daily at an hour that suits the people, it is Sunday Mass that assumes special importance. The Eucharistic celebration on the Lord's Day is the major weekly event at which the parish community gathers before the Lord to adore him, to give thanks, to ask for pardon for sins, and to make other requests, spiritual and temporal. Everything that has to do with the celebration, be it in readings, sacred music, altar equipment, or seating accommodation for the people, should be carefully and lovingly provided. The homily should be such that the people want to come again and eagerly look forward to the next occasion.

Every parish priest is bound by Church law to apply the Sunday Mass for the people entrusted to his pastoral care (cf. *CIC*, can. 534).

The Catholic faith is shown also in the way that the Holy Eucharist is reverenced outside the celebration of Mass. Canon law goes into considerable detail in prescribing the prominent place that the tabernacle should occupy and in describing ways of adoring our Eucharistic Lord (cf. *CIC*, cann. 934–40). The tabernacle should be placed in a prominent and conspicuous place conducive to prayer. Regrettably, in some church buildings set up after the Second Vatican Council, the tabernacle is so hidden away that one could lament with Mary Magdalen: "They have taken the Lord out of the tomb, and we do not know where they have laid him" (Jn 20:2). If a diocese has a well-informed liturgical and building commission with the authority to approve the plans for new churches and the retouching of the sanctuary area of existing churches, this type of mistake can be avoided in every parish.

The Sacrament of the Holy Eucharist continues to exist after the celebration of Holy Mass. The Church, therefore, down through the centuries, has, for instance, in the Latin Rite developed many forms of Eucharistic veneration outside Mass. The consecrated Hosts are reserved in the tabernacle so that Christ can be brought to the sick in their homes or in the hospital, so that people can make visits to the church or chapel to adore, thank, or simply show love for the Lord, and so that Eucharistic Benediction and processions can be facilitated. The Church encourages the holding of hours of adoration of the Holy Eucharist (cf. *CIC*, cann. 941–43). "Wherever possible", says Pope Benedict XVI, "it would be appropriate, especially in densely populated areas, to set aside specific churches or oratories for perpetual adoration" (*Sacramentum Caritatis*, 67). A happy development in many parishes of Nigeria is that the setting up of an adoration chapel, distinct from the parish church, is becoming the normal practice. The parish priest should also celebrate the Eucharistic Benediction for the people on Sundays. Dioceses can organize a Eucharistic congress from time to time. So can the bishops' conference arrange one on the national level at stated periods. The universal Church holds an international Eucharistic congress every four years. A zealous parish priest will work out with his parishioners what part they can play in these congresses, which do much to nourish the faith.

Some dioceses around the world have introduced the service of extraordinary ministers of Holy Communion. These are lay faithful or religious Brothers or Sisters whom the diocesan bishop approves to help the priests in the distribution of the Holy Eucharist. The ordinary ministers of Holy Communion are bishops, priests, deacons, and installed acolytes. When the numbers of the communicants are so high that these ordinary ministers are not enough to administer the Holy Eucharist in a reasonable time at Mass, then the extraordinary ministers can be allowed to help. The aim of approving these extraordinary ministers of Holy Communion is not to promote the status of the laity or the religious. It is therefore a misunderstanding and an abuse when these extraordinary ministers are allowed to distribute Holy Communion while there are only a few communicants or when the ordinary ministers are available in sufficient numbers. The purification of the sacred vessels after Mass is to be done by the ordinary ministers only. It goes without saying that the extraordinary ministers need due formation on the theology of the Holy Eucharist and on the rules for its distribution.

Every parish priest will give maximum attention to whatever concerns the Catholic faith on the Holy Eucharist, on the celebration of this Sacrifice in the parish, and on the adoration due to our Eucharistic Lord outside Mass.

The other sacraments also have their importance in the life of the evangelizing parish. Only a brief word will be said on each of them here.

The parish priest has to see that babies are baptized

in due time. It will be noticed that the occasion of the Baptism of a child is a golden opportunity for the parish priest to make contact with the parents of the child. Some of these parents may no longer attend Sunday Mass regularly. Some may be living in irregular unions without marriage in the Church. Discussion with the priest is obviously very salutary.

Every diocese has its custom about the time for Confirmation. The parish priest will pay attention to it. He will seek ways of maintaining the interest of young people in Church events after they have been confirmed.

Care is needed to prepare children for their First Confession, which should precede their First Communion. The priest should not listen to the theories of those who want children to be admitted to First Communion without First Confession, for the Church has not approved this. While every parish priest is not expected to sit in the confessional for twelve hours each day, like Saint John Mary Vianney, patron of parish priests, it is a sign of a zealous parish priest that he never refuses to hear the confession of a person who makes the request. Every confessor also notes that in the confessional he comes into close contact with an individual soul. There he can give salutary advice and encouragement that the penitent is not likely to get elsewhere. A good confessor is carrying out a very important act of evangelization.

On the Anointing of the Sick, the one remark that cannot be omitted here is that the priest is to convince his people to call the priest to anoint the sick in good time and not wait until death is certain. This sacrament "is not a sacrament for those only who are at the point of death. Hence, as soon as any one of the faithful begins to be in danger of death from sickness or old age, the fitting time for him to receive this sacrament has certainly already arrived" (*Sacrosanctum Concilium*, 73). The more frequently the anointed sick die soon after the priest's visit, the less inclined people will be to call the priest when their dear one is sick until they are certain that he is about to die.

This book cannot go into detail about the pastoral care of people preparing for marriage, of couples already married, and of marriages that are facing the threat of divorce. Every parish priest knows that evangelization must give great attention to the family, which the Second Vatican Council calls "the domestic church" (*Lumen Gentium*, 11).

With respect to Holy Orders, the parish priest contributes best by his life and example, by his careful training of boys as altar servers, by his promotion of priestly vocations, and by his attention to seminarians on holidays or during the period of their practical work in parishes.

Other elements of the sacred liturgy that require the attention of the parish are the Liturgy of the Hours and the celebration of the sacramentals. While clerics and the religious are bound to pray the Divine Office, or Liturgy of the Hours, each day, for the lay faithful these prayers are recommended but are not obligatory. The Second Vatican Council puts it this way: "Pastors of souls should see to it that the chief hours, especially Vespers, are celebrated in common in church on Sundays and the more solemn feasts. And the laity, too, are encouraged to recite the divine office, either with the priests, or among themselves, or even individually" (*Sacrosanctum Concilium*, 100).

The sacred liturgy of the Church has beautiful rites for the consecration of religious men and women, for the dedication of churches, and for the blessing of persons, places, and objects. Most of these blessings in the Roman Ritual are carried out by priests. If priests conduct these rites with due devotion, they are evangelizing.

Marian veneration has an honored place in the parish that evangelizes. "The sacred liturgy does not exhaust the entire activity of the Church" (*Sacrosanctum Concilium*, 9), nor does it cover the entire prayer life of the parish. There has also to be room for popular devotions. "Popular devotions of the Christian people are to be highly commended, provided they accord with the laws and norms of the Church" (*Sacrosanctum Concilium*, 13). Prayer to the patron saint of the parish is one of these devotions. But a special place has to be given to Marian devotion.

In the history of salvation, Divine Providence has assigned a prominent role to the Most Blessed Virgin Mary. Chosen as the Mother of the Incarnate Word, Mary of Nazareth was preserved from original sin and was never under the power of the Evil One. All holy, ever virgin, she was the handmaid of the Lord and Associate of Jesus, the Savior of all humanity.

Marian devotion is therefore a normal part of the Christian life. All generations will call Mary blessed (cf. Lk 1:48). In the Latin Rite, some of the common expressions of devotion to the Immaculate Mother are the Hail Mary, the Holy Rosary, and the wearing of the Scapular. There are also special prayers to her in the month of May, in the Litany of Loreto, and in pilgrimages to approved Marian sanctuaries such as Lourdes, Fatima, Aparecida, Guadalupe, Czestochowa, La Salette, Walsingham, Pompei, and Loreto.

There are many books on Marian devotion that illustrate the scriptural and dogmatic foundations of this practice and also document the lives and examples of saints, such as Saint Louis Grignion Marie de Montfort and Saint Alphonsus Liguori, who were remarkably devoted to the Blessed Mother. It will be helpful for each parish to make such publications easily available to the people. In this connection, I can mention my recent book, *Marian Veneration: Firm Foundations*. The parish priest will also not neglect to give due attention and support to approved Catholic associations that are known for their Marian devotion. Examples are the Legion of Mary, the Children of Mary Sodality, the Block Rosary Association of the Blessed Virgin Mary, Marian sodalities and the Militia of the Immaculata.

Jesus, the Son of God, took on human nature and broke into human history "for us men and for our salvation" (*Credo*). It was through the Virgin Mary that our Savior came to us. On Calvary, Jesus gave his Blessed Mother to Saint John to be his mother. Saint John represents all followers of Christ. The parish that strives to lead people to Christ and to show them how to witness to Christ will best bring them to Christ and teach them to evangelize by going through Mary. Mary leads to Christ. The evangelizing parish has to have an honored place for Marian devotion. Pope Francis sets a good example by his visit to the Basilica of Saint Mary Major in Rome before and after each of his apostolic journeys.

Personal prayer has an important place in the evangelization activity of a parish. The habit of offering personal prayer should not be presumed. It has to be learned. In actual fact, many Catholics are more accustomed to liturgical prayer and to recited non-liturgical prayer, with or without other people. Regretfully, many Catholics do not have the habit or practice of personal prayer, of that prayer that wells up from the heart of the individual, sometimes without words. For many, to pray is to read a prayer that has the text already written out. This in itself is good. For the sacred liturgy, it is obligatory for the text to be already written out, fixed, and approved by the Church. Also for communal non-liturgical group prayer, the text is fixed. Such is the case, for example, with the Legion of Mary prayers, with the Divine Mercy devotion, or with the Rosary.

In addition to liturgical prayer and community prayers, it is necessary for the parish priest and his assistant priests to initiate the lay faithful into a third form of prayer, personal prayer. Here are examples of when such a prayer is indicated. When a person has just received Holy Communion, he does not need a prayer book to speak to Jesus. When a person gets up in the morning or is about to start a journey or finds himself confronted with danger, the person can and should offer a prayer from the heart. Sometimes at the start of a meeting of people from differing Christian families, a person is called upon to offer a prayer in the name of all. The proper thing to do in such a situation is to construct a Christian prayer to which all the participants can subscribe. The person, for example, could pray thus: "Lord God, you have brought us together. We beg you to give us your light and your strength, that we may see what is best for our community (or town or village or state) and that we be united in making a decision that will help solve our problems. Bless those who lead us, guide us all in your ways, and save us from all evil. This we ask of you, through Christ our Lord." Most people will say "Amen" to such a prayer. When children are about to leave home on a long journey or to go to boarding school or when they return home after being away for some months, it is desirable for the parents to pray over them with a prayer composed on the spot. When the members of a family gather around the dinner table or when a family member is celebrating a birthday or an anniversary, what prevents the father or mother from formulating a beautiful prayer for the occasion?

If Catholics do not offer a personal prayer on such or similar occasions, might it not be because they have not been instructed and encouraged to do this? Parishes that want to evangelize need to pay attention to this need. Catholic Bible reading groups and Catholic charismatic renewal groups can be of help. People can be taught how to read a text of Holy Scripture, meditate on it, and then pray to God with this background in their own words. Priests will find that the gatherings of various parish or other social groups are also suitable places to introduce this practice. It is a question of prayers that are not liturgical.

Priests and religious Brothers and Sisters should not regard mental prayer as their special reserve. It would be beautiful if laypeople could also be introduced to this form of personal prayer. They can be helped to see how to read a text of Holy Scripture, for example, and then reflect and pray on it in their hearts. No matter what distractions a person may have, it is always useful to recall that the four major kinds of prayer are adoration, thanksgiving, asking pardon for sins, and making other requests, spiritual and temporal. Even if a person begins with five or ten minutes of daily mental prayer, that would be a good start. With more progress, a person can arrive at half an hour of daily mental prayer, as spiritual masters advise.

It is also to be noted that progress in personal prayer helps the individual to take part in liturgical prayer and in community prayer in a more authentic way. The Roman Missal prescribes several moments of silence in and around the Eucharistic celebration. For example, concelebrants are expected to observe silence in the sacristy and in the procession to the altar, and some moments of silence are recommended after the readings, after the homily, when people have received Holy Communion, and after Mass. The aim is to create a favorable climate for personal prayer. Every parish priest can ask himself how far he has progressed in personal prayer and what he has done to help his people to pray to God from their hearts.

～

6

The Parish Opening Out

A parish, by nature, is missionary. It opens out. It does not fold in upon itself. Jesus sent his disciples: "Go into all the world and preach the gospel to the whole creation" (Mk 16:15). A parish is expected to look out in a dynamic way for what it can do for Christ. It does not settle down to a type of ordinary management pastoral activity, to a type of business as usual method. Rather, it is called to launch out into the deep. There are in most parishes people who have not yet been reached with the Good News of salvation in Jesus Christ in a way that changes their lives. There are lapsed Christians waiting to be contacted. There are people influenced by a secular culture who need the liberating light of the Gospel. There are poor people or the sick who will welcome someone to show them love in the name of Christ. Pope Benedict XVI stresses that a "missionary outreach is a clear sign of the maturity of an ecclesial community. . . . The Church must go out to meet each person in the strength of the Spirit (cf. 1 Cor 2:5) and continue her prophetic defense of people's right and freedom to hear the word of God, while constantly seeking out the most effective ways of proclaiming that word, even at the risk of persecution" (*Verbum Domini*, 95).

This going forth to give witness to Christ can disturb one's personal comfort. Readiness to make sacrifices for the kingdom of Christ is part of what is required of the evangelizer. Pope Francis emphasizes the point: "Each Christian and every community must discern the path that the Lord points out, but all of us are asked to obey his call to go forth from our own comfort zone in order to reach all the 'peripheries' in need of the light of the Gospel" (*Evangelii Gaudium*, 20).

An outgoing parish is not afraid to get involved in the lives of others, to share their concerns, and to try to meet some of their needs. Pope Francis, who is known for his concern for the poor and the needy, insists:

> An evangelizing community knows that the Lord has taken the initiative, he has loved us first (cf. 1 Jn 4:19), and therefore we can move forward, boldly take the initiative, go out to others, seek those who have fallen away, stand at the crossroads and welcome the outcast. Such a community has an endless desire to show mercy, the fruit of its own experience of the power of the Father's infinite mercy. . . . An evangelizing community gets

involved by word and deed in people's daily lives; it
bridges distances, it is willing to abase itself if necessary, and it embraces human life, touching the suffering flesh of Christ in others. (*Evangelii Gaudium*,
24)

This means that the parish community is to be
"permanently in a state of mission" (*Evangelii Gaudium*, 25). It is ever engaged in the work of the Lord.
It is never tired or retired. The Second Vatican Council exhorts pastors: "The care of souls should always be infused with a missionary spirit so that it
reaches out as it should to everyone living within
the parish boundaries. If the pastor cannot contact
certain groups of people, he should seek the assistance of others, even laymen, who can assist him in
the apostolate" (*Christus Dominus*, 30).

It is not too much to expect the parish to show
interest in the worldwide mission of the Church.
An able parish priest will know how to keep the
vision of the parish properly focused on such matters. An example is good information on the work of
the Pontifical Mission Societies (the Society for the
Propagation of the Faith, the Society of Saint Peter
the Apostle, the Holy Childhood Association, and
the Pontifical Missionary Union). A diocesan or national bishops' conference official is usually the person who makes contact with parish priests on such
matters. There is, for example, the Mission Sunday

celebration every October, the Holy Father's Peter's Pence collection in June, or the collection for the Church in the Holy Land on Good Friday. A prudent and missionary-minded parish priest will know how to help his parishioners be well informed on such dimensions of our worldwide mission.

The lay faithful are not to regard evangelizing as primarily the task of clerics and religious. The laity have their full share and responsibility, as has already been indicated in earlier pages. Canon law reminds them: "All the Christian faithful have the duty and the right to work so that the divine message of salvation may increasingly reach the whole of humankind in every age and in every land" (*CIC*, can. 211). "Since the entire Church is missionary by its nature and since the work of evangelization is to be viewed as a fundamental duty of the people of God, all the Christian faithful, conscious of their own responsibility in this area, are to assume their own role in missionary work" (*CIC*, can. 781).

A pastor who is accustomed to one way of conducting the parish apostolate may feel uncomfortable at this suggestion to launch out into deep water. Fear of possible difficulties and mistakes and the raising of new and unforeseen problems may restrain him from a fresher approach. To such a pastor, Pope Francis has this assurance to give:

I prefer a Church which is bruised, hurting and dirty because it has been out on the streets, rather than a Church which is unhealthy from being confined and from clinging to its own security. I do not want a Church concerned with being at the center and which then ends by being caught up in a web of obsessions and procedures. If something should rightly disturb us and trouble our consciences, it is the fact that so many of our brothers and sisters are living without the strength, light and consolation born of friendship with Jesus Christ, without a community of faith to support them, without meaning and a goal in life. More than by fear of going astray, my hope is that we will be moved by the fear of remaining shut up within structures which give us a false sense of security. (*Evangelii Gaudium*, 49)

It follows that the success of a parish priest should not be based primarily on how many buildings he constructed in the parish, on how many structures and committees he set up, or on how much money he generated, nor should it be based on how efficient a manager he was in running parish accounts. While there is no question of refusing to recognize the usefulness of such accomplishments as preparations or scaffoldings for evangelization in the strict sense, the real measure of success for the best parish priest is the number of souls he has led to God, the degree to which he has helped people in the parish become holy Christians, the number of lapsed Catholics he has influenced to return to active practice of the faith, the number of poor people who have seen in him a visible sign of God's love for them, the number of people who see him as their spiritual father, and the number who will shed sincere tears at the announcement of his death.

The rest of this chapter will be an effort to chart out some of the ways in which the parish can launch out into the deep.

Encouragement of people who struggle is one of the marks of a dynamic parish. There are people who are faced with family problems and who need somebody to listen to them and give advice. There are parishioners who are struggling to live up to the demands of the Ten Commandments and who expect, not condemnation, but understanding and help. Drug addicts and alcoholics have different problems. There are other parishioners who need the help that the community can give in fulfilling their desire to give greater attention to Holy Scripture or to become more deeply involved in serving the poor or refugees. Widows and unemployed people are not lacking. What a young person needs most may be a dynamic Catholic youth association.

All such people need to find in the parish a community that encourages, elevates, and gives the individual a sense of belonging. The early Church after the Resurrection of Christ was remarkable for its sense of connectedness. "The company of those who believed", says the Acts of the Apostles, "were of one heart and soul" (Acts 4:32). The small ecclesial communities and the new ecclesial movements and associations mentioned above can be of help.

Stray sheep are to be found in most flocks. Many a parish has parishioners who come to Mass only at Christmas, Easter, weddings, and funerals. There may be couples who were not married in the Church. Superstition does attract some Catholics, so much so that some Catholics can be called "baptized, but not converted". There may be some who are disappointed with the performance of some Church official and who react by keeping away. Others are actually angry with the parish priest or the parish council. Some Catholics have been influenced by the sects and have begun to live lives of double allegiance, while some others have abandoned the Catholic faith altogether. Occasionally one meets Catholics who lament that their parish priest talks too often about money and who respond by boycotting parish celebrations. And what shall we say of people who because of sheer financial problems keep away from the parish church?

A parish cannot remain unconcerned regarding all such people. Someone has to approach them in the name of the parish. If the parish priest cannot do it in some cases, what of his assistant priests, the religious Brothers and Sisters in the parish, and the lay faithful, alone or in groups? Someone has to reconnect with them and give them a sense of belonging. Where the best solution goes beyond what that individual can offer, it should be possible to refer back to the parish priest, who will not fail to know where to turn for help. If someone has kept away from the parish church for a long time, and no one has noticed this or approached him in the name of the parish, then one cannot avoid the conclusion that the parish has still a long way to go in being outgoing.

Propose the Gospel to people who do not yet believe in Christ. This has to be given great priority by the parish. Even in countries evangelized many centuries ago, there may yet be some people who do not believe in Christ. In some parts of the world, such people are still a sizeable number, if not the majority. It is true that the Catholic Church promotes dialogue with the followers of other religions. But such dialogue should not be interpreted to mean that the Gospel is no longer to be proposed to people who do not yet know Jesus Christ. The duty and the necessity to evangelize remain unchanged. "Woe to me

if I do not preach the gospel!" (1 Cor 9:16), Saint
Paul wrote to the Corinthians.

It is necessary in this connection to distinguish
between evangelization and proselytism. They are
different concepts. Proselytism is the effort to get a
person to embrace a religion by the use of unworthy
means such as pressure that is political, economic, financial, social, cultural, or otherwise. This is wrong.
Religion should be an offering made by a free human
being to God the Creator. It should not be forced on
any human being. The human person has the right
to religious freedom. Proselytism is to be rejected.

The proposal of the Gospel to a human being who
enjoys the freedom to accept it or not is evangelization. This is an obligation of the Church that Christ
sent to evangelize and that is therefore by nature missionary. Blessed Paul VI, in his Apostolic Exhortation on Evangelization in the Modern World, speaks
indeed of respect for the followers of other religions
and the need of dialogue with them and then adds
significantly: "Neither respect and esteem for these
religions nor the complexity of the questions raised
is an invitation to the Church to withhold from these
non-Christians the proclamation of Jesus Christ.
On the contrary the Church holds that these multitudes have the right to know the riches of the mystery of Christ—riches in which we believe that the
whole of humanity can find, in unsuspected fullness,

everything that it is gropingly searching for concerning God, man and his destiny, life and death, and truth" (*Evangelii Nuntiandi*, 53; cf. also *Ecclesia in Africa*, 47).

It is to be lamented that there are quite a number of people who are not yet Christians who are living or working in countries regarded as Christian but who are never approached by the parish for a free announcement of the Gospel. An evangelizing parish will remedy this defect where it exists.

Ecumenism is one of the apostolates on which the Church sets high value (cf. *Unitatis Redintegratio*, 1). The division between Christians is against the will of Christ. Regarding his followers, Jesus prayed to his Eternal Father "that they may all be one; even as you, Father, are in me, and I in you" (Jn 17:21). Major initiatives in the promotion of ecumenism will generally be set at the level of the diocese. Each parish can contribute by having contact with other Christians in the area, gestures of friendship with them, and the promotion of certain joint projects. On the choice of marriage partners, parish priests should explain to young people the key importance of religion in life and the need to consider how religion should help a family to pray together and educate the children in the faith of their parents. This will help the young people to appreciate why it would be best if their marriage partner were of the Catholic faith. Where a marriage has actually taken place between a Catholic and a person of another Christian family, the parish priest will not neglect his duty to be near the couple, to see that the Catholic partner remains free to practice the faith, and to look into the Catholic upbringing of the children.

Interreligious dialogue was given considerable attention by the Second Vatican Council. Since all men and women have the same God as Creator, since they form one human community, since Divine Providence has the same final end for them all, and since Jesus Christ is the one and only Savior for all mankind, the Church must pay attention to every human being. If a person who is not a Christian freely welcomes the proclamation of the Gospel, the Church engages in catechesis with a view to Baptism. But if that person does not want to become a Christian, the Church does not thereby lose interest in that person. The Church therefore exhorts Catholics "that through dialogue and collaboration with the followers of other religions, carried out with prudence and love and in witness to the Christian faith and life, they recognize, preserve, and promote the good things, spiritual and moral, as well as the sociocultural values found among these men" (*Nostra Aetate*, 2).

The parish has to see what is possible in this area. There may be followers of other religions whom some Christians can meet at the level of daily life, without any attempt to discuss religion. Friendship can lead to the discovery of some local project that can be jointly promoted. The parish will profit from suggestions from the diocesan office. While conversion to Christianity is not the aim of interreligious dialogue, it is not excluded, because God's grace can move people in directions not foreseen in the beginning of contacts. What is required of the Christian is sincere love and esteem for the other person and authentic witness to Christ in all that concerns relations with other travelers in the pilgrimage that is life on earth.

The poor have traditionally been given great attention by the Church. The parish that wants to be evangelizing gives service to the poor high priority. Think of people who are homeless or whose houses fall below the minimum of what human dignity would indicate. There are people who do not know where their next meal will come from or who depend on begging on the street to keep alive. There are those who are scantily clothed and even some who die of cold in winter. Another type of poverty is found in people who are not able to pay their hospital fees, parents who have to withdraw their children from school for financial reasons, or parents who are embarrassed because they are unable to provide for the adequate clothing and feeding of their children. There are refugees and displaced people and also unemployed youth who lack what is necessary for decent human existence. One can also think of street children and of women made victims of prostitution.

While there is no suggestion here that all such situations of poverty can be resolved by the parish, there is no doubt that an evangelizing Catholic community can be tested by its attitude to the poor and by the measures it takes to meet them and show them Christian love. Jesus has clearly told us that what we do to the least of his brethren we do to him (cf. Mt 25:31–46). Pope Francis says that "each individual Christian and every community is called to be an instrument of God for the liberation and promotion of the poor, and for enabling them to be fully a part of society" (*Evangelii Gaudium*, 187).

Holy Scripture tells us how much God loves the poor. When God saw the suffering of the people of Israel in Egypt, he sent Moses to deliver them. Sirach advises attention to the needy: "Do not avert your eye from the needy, nor give a man occasion to curse you; for if in bitterness of soul he calls down a curse upon you, his Creator will hear his prayer" (Sir 4:5–6). "Water extinguishes a blazing fire: so almsgiving

atones for sin" (Sir 3:30). The angel Raphael tells
the Tobit family: "Almsgiving delivers from death,
and it will purge away every sin" (Tob 12:9). Jesus
preached that "blessed are the poor in spirit, for theirs
is the kingdom of heaven" and "blessed are the merciful, for they shall obtain mercy" (Mt 5:3, 7). The
multitudes were following him and had nothing to
eat and he said to his Apostles: "You give them something to eat" (Mk 6:37). And of course he multiplied
five loaves and two fish and fed thousands. Jesus ex-
plained in Nazareth that he was anointed to preach
Good News to the poor (cf. Lk 4:18). He praised
the poor widow who put just two copper coins into
the temple treasury (cf. Lk 21:2; Mk 12:42). The
poor man Lazarus dies and is carried to the bosom
of Abraham instead of the rich man who used to
banquet every day and paid no attention to the poor
man (cf. Lk 16:19–31). Jesus advised the rich ruler,
who asked him what more he could do to be perfect,
to sell all he had and distribute to the poor, and he
would have treasure in heaven (cf. Lk 18:18–22). To
Judas and anybody else who thought that too much
expense was being made in anointing Christ with
costly ointment, Jesus drew attention to the fact that
occasions to help the poor were always available to
them: "The poor you always have with you, but you
do not always have me" (Jn 12:8; cf. also Mt 26:11;
Mk 14:7). The early Christian community paid great

attention to the poor. The Jerusalem leaders, Peter, James, and John, in commending the missionary travels of Paul and Barnabas, reminded these evangelizers of the Gentiles to "remember the poor, which very thing I was eager to do" (Gal 2:10), said Saint Paul. James in his epistle warns the Christian assemblies of his time not to honor the rich while forgetting or neglecting the poor. "Has not God chosen those who are poor in the world to be rich in faith and heirs of the kingdom which he has promised to those who love him?" (Jas 2:5).

The parish should therefore hear the cry of the poor. The face of Christ is to be seen in every human being, especially in people who are poor or who are in great need. "We are called to find Christ in them," says Pope Francis, "to lend our voice to their causes, but also to be their friends, to listen to them, to speak for them and to embrace the mysterious wisdom which God wishes to share with us through them" (*Evangelii Gaudium*, 198). Every parish will work out what it can do. Possible initiatives are the offering of free meals, the provision of school fees for the indigent where this applies, a parish collection of good clothing from which the poor can choose, a system to pay hospital fees for those who are unable to do so for themselves, the care of orphans and widows, and even help to families too poor to hold decent weddings or funerals for their dear ones. Some parish councils have found it useful to form social services committees whose assignment is to identify parishioners who are in need and advise the parish council on where action should be taken.

These reflections are not suggesting that the parish can solve all the problems of the poor in the world. There are challenges that can be handled only by the diocese, the national government, or even the wider world. Examples are the relationships between the more developed countries of the world and the poorer countries, the functioning of supranational organizations when they operate in what is popularly called the Third World, and any needed reform of international economic and financial institutions, so that they will better promote equitable relationships with less advanced countries (cf. *Catechism of the Catholic Church*, 2440). Nevertheless, the parish can and should meet the poor people within its area and help them in the name of Christ. It is important to remember the principle that the Second Vatican Council calls the universal destination of earthly goods, the common purpose of created things: "God intended the earth with everything contained in it for the use of all human beings and peoples. Thus, under the leadership of justice and in the company of charity, created goods should be in abundance for all in like manner" (*Gaudium et Spes*, 69). That means that a few people in the world are not to become an oasis of opulence and squandermania, while the majority remain a desert of misery and want. "God gave the earth to the whole human race for the sustenance of all its members, without excluding or favoring anyone" (*Compendium of the Social Doctrine of the Church*, 171).

Pope Francis has a rather harsh warning to give to a parish community that is insensitive to the poor: "Any Church community, if it thinks it can comfortably go its own way without creative concern and effective cooperation in helping the poor to live with dignity and reaching out to everyone, will also risk breaking down, however much it may talk about social issues or criticize governments. It will easily drift into a spiritual worldliness camouflaged by religious practices, unproductive meetings and empty talk" (*Evangelii Gaudium*, 207). The parish that wants to evangelize has to give much attention to the poor.

Service of the sick should be a major commitment of a parish that is dynamically engaged in evangelizing. The teaching of the Lord Jesus is that what we do to and for the sick is done to and for him. This dimension of witnessing to Christ therefore deserves close attention. The sick have a place in God's care in the Old Testament. In the New Covenant, Jesus gives the model approach. The early Church followed his example. The Church today strives to do the same. The parish, therefore, has its route well mapped out.

In the Old Testament, the person who was sick looked up to God for healing, since God is master of life and death. Illness was often regarded as linked to sin and evil, so that conversion with faithfulness to God was considered a means of restoring good health, "For I am the LORD, your healer" (Ex 15:26). The prophet Isaiah speaks of the Lord's suffering servant whose sufferings can have redemptive meaning for the sins of others (Is 53:11). The same prophet announces that God will usher in a time for Zion when he will pardon every offense and heal every illness "and no inhabitant will say, 'I am sick'" (Is 33:24).

Jesus showed great sympathy toward the sick. He healed them, whether they had fever, paralysis, hemorrhage, leprosy, palsy, blindness, or possession by the devil (cf. Mk 6:5; 8:23; Jn 9:1–7). He regarded himself as the physician of whom the sick have need (cf. Mk 2:17). The sick flocked to him for healing. As the Evangelist Luke testifies: "All the crowd sought to touch him, for power came forth from him and healed them all" (Lk 6:19; cf. also Mk 1:41; 3:10; 6:56). Jesus healed so many sick people in Peter's house that the Evangelist Matthew saw in this the fulfillment of the prophecy of Isaiah: "He took our infirmities and bore our diseases" (Mt 8:17; Is 53:4).

There was no doubt about the love that Jesus showed to the sick. As Saint John Paul II puts it: "In his messianic activity in the midst of Israel, Christ drew increasingly closer *to the world of human suffering*. 'He went about doing good', and his actions concerned primarily those who were suffering and seeking help" (*Salvifici Doloris*, 16).

Jesus, however, did not heal all the sick. And he often demanded faith. "His healings were signs of the coming of the Kingdom of God. They announced a more radical healing: the victory over sin and death through his Passover. On the cross Christ took upon himself the whole weight of evil and took away the 'sin of the world' [Jn 1:29; cf. Is 53:4−6], of which illness is only a consequence. By his passion and death on the cross Christ has given a new meaning to suffering: it can henceforth configure us to him and unite us with his redemptive Passion" (*Catechism of the Catholic Church*, 1505).

The Apostles and the early Church obeyed the instruction of Christ to "heal the sick" (Mt 10:8). When Jesus sent his Apostles to preach, "they cast out many demons, and anointed with oil many that were sick and healed them" (Mk 6:13). In the Acts of the Apostles, we are told that Peter in Lydda healed a man who had been bedridden for eight years and was paralyzed. "Peter said to him, 'Aeneas, Jesus Christ heals you; rise and make your bed.' And immediately he rose" (Acts 9:34). The Apostles were well aware that in his commissioning of them just before he ascended into heaven, Jesus had promised that "these signs will accompany those who believe: in my name they will cast out demons. . . . ; they will lay their hands on the sick, and they will recover" (Mk 16:17–18). Saint Paul recognized the charism of healing as one of the gifts of the Holy Spirit (cf. 1 Cor 12:9, 28, 30). Saint James testifies that the early Church had her own special rite for the sick: "Is any among you sick? Let him call for the elders of the Church, and let them pray over him, anointing him with oil in the name of the Lord; and the prayer of faith will save the sick man, and the Lord will raise him up; and if he has committed sins, he will be forgiven" (Jas 5:14–15). "Tradition has recognized in this rite one of the seven sacraments" (*Catechism of the Catholic Church*, 1510), the Anointing of the Sick.

Down through the centuries, the Church has striven to remain faithful to the injunction of Christ to serve the sick. The first hospitals as we know them today arose out of the Christian concern to look after the sick and to welcome strangers. Care centers for people who are ill, old, or handicapped, as well as full-blown hospitals, are in the tradition of the Church. Many religious congregations have been founded for the care of the sick. Indeed, at the level of the universal Church, Saint John Paul II on February 11, 1985, instituted in the Roman Curia a Commission (later called Pontifical Council) for Health Care Workers. This office was on January 1, 2017, merged with three other offices in a new dicastery now known as the Dicastery for Promoting Integral Human Development.

The Church is aware that the Lord Jesus did not heal all the sick. She does not, therefore, forget to share with the sick the Scripture truth that sickness and suffering can have redemptive value when the person who suffers strives to be in union with Christ. Saint Paul learned from the Lord that "My grace is sufficient for you, for my power is made perfect in weakness" (2 Cor 12:9). Paul's appreciation of the redemptive value of suffering made him write to the Colossians: "Now I rejoice in my sufferings for your sake, and in my flesh I complete what is lacking in Christ's afflictions for the sake of his body, that is, the Church" (Col 1:24). On March 12, 2017, Pope Francis said to sick and elderly people in the church of Santa Maddalena di Canossa in Rome: "Illness is a cross—you know this—but the Cross is always a seed of life, and by bearing it well one can give much life to many people whom we do not know; and then, in Heaven, we will know them. I thank you for bearing your illness in this way."

In light of these reflections, it becomes clear what the parish is expected to do in the service of the sick.

Effort should be made to see Christ in the suffering members of humanity, beginning with those of the household of the faith. The parish should begin by identifying the sick, whether in their homes or in hospitals or similar care centers. The social services committee set up by the parish council and individuals charged by the parish priest can help in this. Then it should be arranged who is to visit them in the name of the parish. No matter who does this, a regular visit by the parish priest, or another priest, is a gesture not to be omitted, perhaps once a month. In such a visit, the priest will exchange some suitable conversation with the sick and see which sacramental administration they need. It is suitable and encouraging that at least once a month a priest, a religious Brother or Sister, or an extraordinary minister of Holy Communion brings the sick the Holy Eucharist, by prior arrangement. Visits to the sick will also indicate to the parish how best to be of help. It could be financial help. It might be a link with a doctor or hospital. Or what is needed may be that some young people of the parish should come to the home of the sick to do some laundry, some general cleaning, or some errands to the supermarket. Parishioners can be well instructed on the need to call the priest to administer the Sacrament of the Anointing of the Sick whenever a person is seriously sick, even if there is no immediate danger of death. The parish

priest could also motivate some wealthy parishioners
to donate money to the parish for help to sick people who are in need. In the service of the sick, the
redemptive value of suffering should be brought to
the attention of the sick in a prudent way. Whoever
has something to suffer has something to offer. Sick
members of the Church are among the jewels of the
Bride of Christ. While the Church prays for them,
they also pray for the Church and the world, and the
merciful Lord will not ignore their prayers.

The evangelizing parish lovingly serves Christ in
the sick.

Home visitation is another important way in which a
parish evangelizes. Generally, it is the parish priest,
possibly in the company of one or two other persons,
who visits the families in his parish. Once a year is
considered usual. The parishioners are informed in
good time. The visit is not meant just for the families of the best Christians: it is a systematic visit to
all families, whether they are fervent in the practice
of the faith or not. The parish is generally divided
into zones so that the pastoral visit systematically
covers one zone after the other. It is important that
the visit not raise any embarrassment to poor families who may worry about what they should offer
the priest. It is best for the parish priest to announce
to the people in church that the only gift he will

accept is a glass of drinking water. In a country like Nigeria, the offer of kola nuts may be demanded by the local culture. The main concern on this point is that the visit should be one in which no gifts are expected. During the visit, the pastor listens to the members of the family, and the conversation has no rigid laws of subjects for discussion. Obviously the priest is interested in how the family is getting on in the practice of the faith. But questions on social, cultural, or financial problems are not excluded. When the parish priest has no ready answer, it is quite in order for him to promise the family to refer the matter to others who can be of help. Some matters discussed could be delicate, and discretion is no doubt needed on the part of the priest. He does not visit as an ecclesiastical inquisitor or Church police officer. He comes as a pastor who wants to be at the disposal of his people for a cordial exchange. The visit can be concluded with the blessing of everyone by the priest.

The Second Vatican Council stresses the importance of such home visitation:

> In fulfilling their office of shepherd, pastors should take pains to know their own flock. Since they are the servants of all the sheep, they should encourage a full Christian life among the individual faithful and also in families, in associations especially dedicated to the apostolate, and in the whole parish

community. Therefore, they should visit homes and schools to the extent that their pastoral work demands. They should pay special attention to adolescents and youth. They should devote themselves with a paternal love to the poor and the sick. They should have a particular concern for workingmen. Finally, they should encourage the faithful to assist in the works of the apostolate. (*Christus Dominus*, 30)

This shows how much the Church treasures the nearness of the priest to his people.

The 1983 *Code of Canon Law* echoes these expressed concerns of the council regarding parish pastoral visits:

In order to fulfill his office in earnest the pastor should strive to come to know the faithful who have been entrusted to his care; therefore he is to visit the families, sharing the cares, worries, and especially the griefs of the faithful, strengthening them in the Lord, and correcting them prudently if they are wanting in certain areas; with a generous love he is to help the sick, particularly those close to death, refreshing them solicitously with the sacraments and commending their souls to God; he is to make a special effort to seek out the poor, the afflicted, the lonely, those exiled from their own land, and similarly those weighed down with special difficulties; he is also to labor diligently so that spouses and parents are supported in fulfilling their

proper duties, and he is to foster growth in the
Christian life within the family. (*CIC*, can. 529, §1).

Every parish priest will agree that this job descrip-
tion is formidable and at the same time loving and
comprehensive.

The advantages of a pastoral visit carried out in the
proper manner are not far to seek. It brings priest
and people together better than any number of dis-
cussions in the parish office. It helps the priest to
understand better the challenges and problems the
families may be experiencing and gives him an opportunity to commend them for their successes in
their struggles. The priest will in a prudent way see
how to revise his homilies, so that they relate better
to the harsh realities of daily life in which the people
find themselves and where they are striving to live in
the light of the Gospel. The pastor will also find out
where the parish social services committee or other
experts can be invited to help.

Pope Francis emphasizes how necessary it is for
the pastor to follow the example of Jesus in being
near the lives and needs of the people, entering into
the fabric of society, sharing the lives of the people,
listening to their concerns, helping them materially
and spiritually in their needs, rejoicing with those
who rejoice and weeping with those who weep, in
order to build a new world. He advises the priest
to get involved and not close himself up in the rec-

tory: "Sometimes we are tempted to be that kind of Christian who keeps the Lord's wounds at arm's length. Yet Jesus wants us to touch human misery, to touch the suffering flesh of others. He hopes that we will stop looking for those personal or communal niches which shelter us from the maelstrom of human misfortune and instead enter into the reality of other people's lives and know the power of tenderness. Whenever we do so, our lives become wonderfully complicated and we experience intensely what it is to be a people, to be part of a people" (*Evangelii Gaudium*, 270). The pope uses rather strong words to speak of how necessary it is for a missionary to go out, meet others, and get involved in helping them. To the parish priest who shies away from pastoral visitation, the pope could apply this judgment: "Only the person who feels happiness in seeking the good of others, in desiring their happiness, can be a missionary. This openness of the heart is a source of joy, since 'it is more blessed to give than to receive' (Acts 20:35). We do not live better when we flee, hide, refuse to share, stop giving and lock ourselves up in our own comforts. Such a life is nothing less than slow suicide" (*Evangelii Gaudium*, 272).

The missionary-minded parish priest will not fail to appreciate the importance of well-planned pastoral visits and will make the needed sacrifice to carry them out in the best possible way.

To stay or to quit can be the challenge thrown to a local Catholic community. Here are two examples. In the early days of missionary work in Nigeria, the missionaries considered the negative influences of the traditional African religion and the customs it inspired to be so strong that it was better to withdraw the first Christians from their village community. These new Christians were then relocated in a new village called the Christian village. This new community was built around the mission station church and the priests' house, which were placed at a distance from the people's traditional village. The aim was to save the new Christians from contamination with what the missionaries saw as pagan surroundings and customs.

A second example of an attempt to quit is offered by what happened in one Catholic community in the United States of America. Some of the Catholics in a town considered the society in which they lived to be increasingly secular; values found in the society were negative from the religious point of view; the public approach to sexuality, marriage, and the family was not in line with the Christian faith; and freedom of religion was sometimes menaced. With society so hostile to religion, it was getting more difficult to educate children in the faith. Some of the Catholics, therefore, proposed the idea that it would be better for them to relocate and go to live near a monastery that was some distance from the town.

The general comment on these two attempts to live the Christian faith by going away from the actual society is that, while there is no denying the power of the challenges in the two situations just sampled, another and more dynamic solution has to be sought. In the first case, the missionaries have to appreciate that the Gospel is meant to work as leaven in society. The first Christians have to find a way to give witness to Christ in the actual society where they live and work. No matter the initial difficulties, the seed that is the word of God will eventually sprout from the local ground by divine watering. Gradually the Christian life will sprout, and a Christian community will emerge. When Jesus sent his first disciples to evangelize the world, there were no Christian communities. The challenges posed by society were formidable. But the disciples did not quit. And the missionaries in African countries have succeeded in forming local Churches that eventually bring the best of their people's cultures to enrich the living of the Gospel (cf. *Ad Gentes*, 22). Today we are accustomed to stressing the importance of inculturation, of the Gospel being incarnated in the local culture, and of every evangelized people being at home in the Church (cf. *Ecclesia in Africa*, 59).

In response to the proposal that Catholic families in a country evangelized for centuries should leave a secularistic society in order to go and live near a monastery, we can begin by showing appreciation for some of their gains: they will enjoy a strong sense of community; they will have beautiful liturgical celebrations in the monastery; the education of their children in the faith will pose fewer problems in their new Catholic community; and the Catholics will know each other and find it easier to share joys and sorrows. There are, however, worrying questions to be answered. Are these Catholics not abandoning the call to evangelize society? Do these Catholics want to live the monastic life? Are they not by their departure declaring themselves good people and the rest of society bad? How are their children going to fit into their country as citizens? How can they evangelize society as insiders now that they have pulled themselves out of it?

There is no doubt that the monastic life is very precious to the Church. Monks and nuns, like Saint Benedict, abandon the world in order to live in monastic enclosures and seek closer union with God. Writing on forms of the contemplative life, Pope Benedict XVI declares: "I think in particular of monks and cloistered nuns, who by virtue of their separation from the world are all the more closely united to Christ, the heart of the world. More than ever, the Church needs the witness of men and women resolved to 'put nothing before the love of Christ' [Saint Benedict: *Rule*, IV, 21]" (*Verbum Domini*, 83). Monastic enclosure has traditionally included some form of physical separation from the ordinary society in which most people live.

The vocation of the lay faithful, and therefore of the Christian family, is different from the monastic calling. The apostolate specific to the lay faithful is the evangelization of the secular sphere of life. It is their vocation to bring the spirit of Christ into marriage and the family, the place of work and recreation, trade and commerce, politics and government, national and international relations (cf. *Lumen Gentium*, 36–38; *Apostolicam Actuositatem*, 2, 7). This implies their living in the normal society and acting within it as leaven. Leaven in dough acts from within. This is why what has above been called "departure" is not a proper solution. The lay faithful can indeed visit monasteries. It is very beneficial for them to do so. They can go to monasteries for spiritual retreats, for spiritual consultation, and to benefit from an atmosphere of silence and from beautiful liturgical celebrations. But, thereafter, they return to the secular world that is their specific area of apostolate.

These reflections lead to the question of how the parish should behave toward the society in which it finds itself. Jesus said to his disciples: "Put out into the deep and let down your nets for a catch" (Lk 5:4). The parish has to confess Christ in the public square. It should meet the men and women of today where they are and then strive to bring them to Christ the Savior. No matter the difficulties and challenges posed by the evangelization of society, the proper answer should not be to leave. If the early Church had not launched out into the deep, then Christianity would not have spread. "If I can help at least one person to have a better life," says Pope Francis, "that already justifies the offering of my life. It is a wonderful thing to be God's faithful people. We achieve fulfilment when we break down walls and our heart is filled with faces and names!" (*Evangelii Gaudium*, 274).

Other evangelizers are at work. The parish should not only not ignore them, but should seek ways in which it can work together with them in the service of the Gospel.

To begin with, there are other parishes, and there is the diocese. There are many demands and services of the apostolate that go beyond one parish and require the cooperation of several parishes. Sometimes it is the diocese that is called upon to lay down a policy, to approve a lay apostolate association, or to appoint a chaplain to one such organization that functions in several parishes. It is the duty of the leaders in all the parishes involved to see that petty jealousy and envy are not allowed to dissipate apostolic energy.

Religious Brothers and Sisters are a happy reality in any parish. These men and women are striving to follow Christ with a radical commitment concretized in the three evangelical counsels of chastity, poverty, and obedience. Their living of their consecration is already an evangelizing act. According to their various charisms, some of these religious live lives of striking simplicity; others have specialized in teaching; some in medical and social services; others in primary evangelization in mission situations; some in the conducting of spiritual retreats for groups; others in rescuing street children or trafficked women; and some in the promotion of special devotions like devotion to the Sacred Heart or to the Divine Mercy. A wise parish priest will find a way to associate these religious in the parish apostolate and allow the parishioners to reap rich benefits from the presence and operation of these consecrated people and to be challenged by their radicalism in the following of Christ. Some religious Brothers or Sisters may be new in a parish, or they may stand in need of some form of material help that the parish can provide.

If a parish has lay faithful who figure in the diocesan apostolate or in the work of the universal Church by participation in the functioning of some part of the Roman Curia or in the work of Catholic associations on the national or world level, then the parish priest should be glad. He can find a way to include such able laypeople in the parish apostolate. The Second Vatican Council says that the lay faithful should develop an ever-increasing appreciation of their own diocese, of which the parish is a kind of cell, ever ready at their pastor's invitation to participate in diocesan projects. Indeed, to fulfill the needs of cities and rural areas, they should not limit their cooperation to the parochial or diocesan boundaries but strive to extend it to interparochial, interdiocesan, national, and international fields. This is constantly becoming all the more necessary because the daily increase in mobility of populations, reciprocal relationships, and means of communication no longer allow any sector of society to remain closed in upon itself. Thus they should be concerned about the needs of the people of God dispersed throughout the world. (*Apostolicam Actuositatem*, 10)

The major point being made here is that the parish, under the leadership of the parish priest, should be aware that there are many other actors in the field of evangelization and that the best results will be achieved when the parish recognizes them and willingly works with them.

Problems and challenges on the road to deeper evangelization are to be found in every parish. The above reflections should not be read as if everything were easy and simple for the parish that wants to be active in witnessing to Christ. These problems and challenges, however, can be identified, and ways can be found to meet them. Here are some of them.

One challenge for some parishes may be that of personnel. There may not be enough priests to serve the vast numbers of people. There may be problems of factionalism among the members of the parish council or disappointment on the part of some who did not obtain the assignment they desired. Some parishes suffer from poor leadership qualities in their parish priest or some member of a parish committee. Such leaders may be short-sighted and rather poor in understanding a situation and working toward a solution. They may not be humble enough to allow themselves to be helped. They may not be willing to call on people better gifted than themselves. Humility, patience, prudence, and realism will be needed on all sides in the search for adequate solutions.

A second challenge can be a lack of proper cohesion between the parishioners. They may be mainly migrants or exiles. They could be neighbors who have settled recently at the peripheries of a growing city and who have not yet begun to function as a harmonious spiritual family. Daily life can be rather difficult for very poor people living in poor and unplanned suburbs outside a big city, chiefly concerned about their daily bread and how to look after their children. However, it is not impossible to fashion a harmonious community even in such deprived surroundings, although much patience and empathy with the poor will be needed on the part of the parish priest and his close assistants.

A parish can be in difficulty because of human weakness that shows itself in sectionalism, tribalism, elitism, and unwillingness on the part of some parishioners to meet others. There may be coldness in welcoming newcomers to the parish or in sharing the concerns of the poor. There is also the question of the selfish parishioner who just wants to attend Sunday Mass but does not want to be bothered by any parish projects or suggested meetings.

Some parishes are too poor through no fault of their own. They may be at the outskirts of a big city. They may not be in a position to build a decent, if humble, church. They may need financial help from the diocesan center or from a parish with greater resources, according to the decision of the bishop. The parishes that are stronger from the financial point of view should not be unwilling to share some of the means that Divine Providence has given them. The bishop may also be able to attract help from the Christians in another country or from a wealthier diocese in the same country.

In some parishes, the problem is a growing bureaucracy. The parish may have grown so much both in population and in the complexity of services it offers that it now has separate directorates for worship, music, catechetics, service of the sick, accounting, and even home visitation. Some of these parish workers may be full-time and need some remuneration at the end of the month. Some measure of division of labor cannot be avoided, especially when the parish has grown rather large. But the parish priest and his assistants have to watch the development of events carefully. The people who are at the head of bureaucratic departments understandably tend to justify the existence of their work. There can be exaggeration when the structure seems to regard itself as more important than the individuals it is meant to serve. Unconsciously provoked incidents of a power struggle between different services, or between their leaders and the parish priest, cannot always be avoided. All parish workers should hold as most dear the spirit bequeathed to us by the Lord Jesus: "Whoever would be great among you must be your servant, and whoever would be first among you must be slave of all. For the Son of man also came not to be served but to serve, and to give his life as a ransom for many" (Mk 10:43–45).

As can be seen, problems and challenges that face the parish are not lacking. But they can be confronted. And they should be.

∽

7

Special Parish Apostolates

The foregoing pages have spelled out how the parish can evangelize. The parish has to be missionary. It is to be outgoing. It is not to be "self-referential", as Pope Francis sometimes puts it. It is not to be closed in upon itself. There are some special apostolates that have not yet been given sufficient attention in this book and that are now to be considered in this closing chapter. One thinks of special parish apostolates to the family, to young people, to the school education of children, to elderly citizens, and to devotional groups. Individual apostolates will be the closing consideration.

The family is that natural society founded on the marriage of a man and a woman. It is where life is procreated and nurtured. It is the cell of society, a "community of love" (*Gaudium et Spes*, 47), "the beginning and basis of human society" (*Apostolicam Actuositatem*, 11), and "the domestic church" (*Lumen Gentium*, 11). The health and condition of the family are of great importance to the health and condition of both the Church and the State.

The parish has to give much attention to the preparation of young people for marriage. Instruction on catechetical, medical, and social matters will be needed. Married couples can be invited to meet engaged couples and give them all the help that their wisdom and experience advise. In some places, costs of wedding celebrations are too expensive for the poor. The parish must ask itself what it can do to help.

There are several family enhancement programs and family promotion apostolates around the world. Examples are the Marriage Encounter apostolate, the Apostolate for Family Consecration, the Couples for Christ, and the Christian Family Movement. Each parish will carefully find out which of them function in its diocese or country and how they can help. What is important is that it should not be presumed that good families need no help. All families do need encouragement, and a good and well-functioning family can be helped to become better and to function at greater heights.

Some families may be in difficulty. There are couples who live in irregular unions without being married in the Church. They need to be helped to overcome their hesitation and to get their union blessed by the Lord and the Church. There are properly married couples who live in tension. Someone in the name of the parish must listen to them with great respect and see what can be done to help them live in that peace and love which the Creator intends for the family. There are some married people who have been abandoned by their spouses and who, perhaps, have to bring up their children singlehandedly. No matter where the fault lies, such people should see that the parish has not forgotten them. There are some people who are divorced and remarried. Even if the fault is on the side of their former spouse, it is clear from the teaching of Jesus that divorce and re-marriage cannot be approved (cf. Mt 5:32; Mk 10:11–12; Lk 16:18). The parish should not abandon such couples. They are not excommunicated. They are to be encouraged to continue to come to Mass, to take part in parish events, and to continue to pray to God for a solution. If any of the spouses involved considers that for some reason the marriage to the divorced partner should be declared invalid from its very start, the proper thing to do is to have recourse to the diocesan office and the bishop. If such a decla-ration comes from a Church court, it will open their way to the sacraments. Whatever the parish can do to help in the Catholic education of the children in-volved in such tragedies will be a duty of Christian charity.

Prayer in the family is an important consideration.

Many families *de facto* do not pray together. The mother in the family could be the person who should gather the other members in the family for night prayers. It is praiseworthy if the family can pray the Holy Rosary together in the evening. Prayers before and after meals should be easier to organize. If the parents are strict on this, the children will be learning lessons that may stay with them all through their lives. Parents have to be convinced that their behavior influences their children more than the parents might realize. The Bible should be permanently enthroned in a prominent place in the family. And the parents are to see that each of their children has a personal copy of at least the New Testament.

The parents are the primary educators of their children. The schoolteachers, the Church, and the State come in to work with the parents. It is for the parish priest to keep reminding parents of their duty to give their children a sound education in the faith and to choose suitable schools for them.

The parish can encourage families to participate in a family apostolate. The more successful and experienced couples can be persuaded to sit with the younger couples from time to time and share experiences with them. Medical doctors, nurses, and social workers who share the pastoral and social doctrine of the Church can occasionally be invited to hold seminars for the younger couples.

Young people occupy an important place in the hearts of their parents and in the life of the Church and the State. They are a gift and a responsibility to their parents, the parish, the diocese, and the State. The parish must have a well-reserved and cared for place for them. It is not enough to call them the leaders of tomorrow. They are a very significant sector of the parish of today.

The parish has to work with the family to help the young people share in the sacramental life of the Church, especially in the Sacraments of Christian Initiation: Baptism, Confirmation, and the Holy Eucharist. The Sacrament of Reconciliation or Penance must be received before the First Communion. And the parish must find a way to keep the young people involved in active participation in the Sunday Mass all through their lives. Adequate organization of catechism classes will be necessary to prepare the young people to receive the sacraments for the first time, while the teaching of the faith to adolescents has to differ from the style of catechism taught to primary school children. As children, the young people can participate in the parish church choir or become altar servers.

Participation in Catholic youth organizations will be found very useful. Most dioceses have approved forms so that the parish does not have to invent one. The young people's "zest for life and a ready eagerness to assume their own responsibility" (*Apostolicam*

Actuositatem, 12) should be positively recognized and encouraged by the parish. Youth want to be involved in social work and assistance of the sick and the elderly, and the parish should afford them ample opportunity to do this.

The parish can help young people in their relationships with adults. As the Second Vatican Council observes: "Adults ought to engage in such friendly discussion with young people that both age groups, overcoming the age barrier, may become better acquainted and share the special benefits each generation can offer the other. . . . By the same token young people should cultivate toward adults respect and trust" (*Apostolicam Actuositatem*, 12).

In our times, the communications media are very much at the disposal of everyone, but especially of the young people, who are often more proficient than their parents in the use of these digital media. The task for young people is to use these media in a disciplined way and not to allow any of them to dominate their lives. This is where the parish can be of help, because spiritual discipline is a virtue to be learned.

The parish can be of help to young people in the choice of a state of life. Most of them will choose to marry. Preparation for marriage should begin even before a young person chooses a marriage partner. With their inexperience, young people can make

many mistakes. They need to be advised about the
possible pitfalls and trained in the virtues of chastity,
honesty, and nobility, which will serve them in good
stead. Priestly and religious vocations should be ex-
plained to young people and put before them as possible calls of Divine Providence. The best people to
do this are priests or religious Brothers or Sisters
who live their vocations with one hundred percent
fidelity and with manifest joy and interior peace. A
parish priest who does not propose any of these ecclesiastical vocations to his young people would be
committing an act of omission. For recruitment of
vocations to the seminary, it has been found that
a devout priest who celebrates the sacred mysteries with transparent joy and fidelity to the liturgical laws and who trains boys as altar servers with
great pastoral care is the best promoter of priestly
vocations. Where the priest is careless at the altar
or nonchalant in the celebration of the other sacraments, the parish will have to lament having a priest
who is discouraging vocations to the sacred priesthood.

A good Christian is a good citizen. The parish
has to educate its young people to love their country and to work out a vital synthesis between their
religious practice and their duties as citizens. The
Second Vatican Council teaches that "the Christian
who neglects his temporal duties neglects his duties

toward his neighbor and even God, and jeopardizes his eternal salvation" (*Gaudium et Spes*, 43). The council continues to underline the importance of the respect due to civic duties: "Great care must be taken about civic and political formation, which is of the utmost necessity today for the population as a whole, and especially for youth, so that all citizens can play their part in the life of the political community" (*Gaudium et Spes*, 75).

As children grow up, they will learn to participate in Catholic youth organizations, not only in the parish and diocese, but also in the nation and even in the universal Church. The World Youth Day that was introduced by Saint John Paul II in 1985 has had an extraordinary power to motivate young people to become more committed to their faith. It is noticed that after every such celebration, there is an upward surge in the number of young people who become better Christians, who prepare more seriously for marriage, or who enter seminaries or religious congregations. The World Youth Day is celebrated on Palm Sunday at the diocesan level, and once in about every three years, it is held at the world level in a city chosen by the Holy Father. A country like Nigeria has introduced the celebration of a National Youth Day one year before the World Youth Day Celebration. In his message to the youth of the world on the occasion of the ninth and tenth World Youth Days,

1994–1995, Saint John Paul II wrote: "I hope that the celebration of these days may be for you all a privileged occasion of formation and growth in the personal and community knowledge of Christ; may it be an interior stimulus to consecrate yourselves to the Church in the service of your brothers and sisters to build the civilization of love" (*Message to IX and X World Youth Days*, 6).

Some young people find themselves in difficult circumstances. Their parents may be divorced. They may be orphans. One of their parents could be in prison. And some young people are unemployed. The parish does not have the means to resolve all these challenges and problems. But it can help. It can find many ways to be near these suffering young people. It can motivate the wealthier parishioners to lend a hand to programs in favor of youth.

The school apostolate has engaged the Church down through the centuries because it is a question of preparing young citizens for full participation in life. The Second Vatican Council says:

> In a special way, the duty of educating belongs to the Church, not merely because she must be recognized as a human society capable of educating, but especially because she has the responsibility of announcing the way of salvation to all men, of communicating the life of Christ to those who believe,

and, in her unfailing solicitude, of assisting men to be able to come to the fullness of this life. The Church is bound as a mother to give to these children of hers an education by which their whole life can be imbued with the spirit of Christ and at the same time do all she can to promote for all peoples the complete perfection of the human person, the good of earthly society and the building of a world that is more human. (Declaration on Christian Education, *Gravissimum Educationis*, 3)

Every diocese has its program for the promotion of Catholic education. The parish will do its best to be part of it. In most dioceses, it is the practice to maintain a Catholic primary school. No parish should neglect this service for the young. The key to success is to have a team of teachers who share strong convictions in accord with the Catholic faith and who are ready not only to teach but also to educate and form the young citizens in the faith. Where possible, the teacher of religion should be a priest or a well-prepared religious or layperson.

Not all children go to a Catholic school. Quite a number study in some type of public or State school. The situation varies around the world. The parish priest should prudently see how the religious education of such children can be provided. Sometimes it is possible to have a Catholic as religion teacher in such schools. Where this is not possible, the parish should look into some Sunday or evening special religion classes for the children.

Elderly people constitute an important and rich constituent of the community, sacred and secular. The parish reserves a loving and respectful place for them.

Sacred Scripture presents the older person as the symbol of someone rich in wisdom and fear of the Lord (cf. Sir 25:4–6). The older person gives witness to what God has done for past generations (cf. Ps 44:1–2; Ex 12:26–27). He is the wise person from whose maxims and proverbs one will gain instruction and learn how to serve great men (cf. Sir 6:34; 8:8).

Certain temptations can assail elderly people. They can feel forgotten or not taken into sufficient account by the younger generation, including young priests and other young parish leaders. For them, society is changing all the time, and the new digital age can be confusing with its many gadgets. Senior citizens can be tempted to praise former times and suspect modern developments, if not even to lose hope that the world of today and the Church of our times can meet the needs of the human person. It is sad when elderly people begin to regard themselves as unproductive or as a burden on the young.

The opportunities open to elderly people are many. With their life experience, they have a better possibility than younger people to evaluate the past, to appreciate more precisely the values that are lasting, and to propose possible solutions. Many younger people and leaders of Church and State are ready to listen to them, even if they do not always accept the conclusions proposed by their elders. Therefore the old should consider themselves, not "as persons underestimated in the life of the Church or as passive objects in a fast-paced world, but as participants at a time of life which is humanly and spiritually fruitful" (*Christifideles Laici*, 48).

There are many ways for the parish to have contact with elderly citizens and show them that they are appreciated. It is not a bad idea for a parish to arrange a special Mass for the elderly, even if it is only once or twice a year. A suitable votive Mass can be chosen if the liturgical rules permit it. One or two of the elderly can read the first reading or the responsorial psalm. The homily can be tailored to suit the occasion. And the Mass can be followed by a simple reception in the parish hall.

A social event in honor of the elderly people in the parish can take various forms. It can be opened with an address from the parish priest and the parish council. A variety concert by young people can follow. Several old people can be chosen to give talks and advice to the young. There can be an opportunity for questions and answers to promote communication between the old and the young. And the whole event can be arranged to deliver the message to the old that they are appreciated, respected, and listened to.

Old age is a gift and a treasure that both Church and State need to appreciate and for which both the old and the young should be grateful.

Devotional groups function in the parish and need understanding, appreciation, and help. They are of differing types. Some of them are associations with the direct aim of honoring some aspect of the mysteries of Christ, like the Society of the Sacred Heart, the Holy Face Association, the Association of the Precious Blood, and the Divine Mercy Devotion. Some are meant to promote devotion to the Blessed Virgin Mary, like the Our Lady of Fatima Association, the Children of Mary Organization, the Scapular, the First Saturdays Devotion, and the Block Rosary Crusade. Other devotional groups honor saints, like Saint Anthony of Padua, Saint Pio of Pietrelcina, Saint Thérèse of Lisieux, and the Blessed Cyprian Michael Tansi Solidarity Movement. There are devotional associations that not only honor the saints but have a defined practical apostolate. Examples are the Legion of Mary, which honors Our Blessed Mother

and has practical home visitation as a weekly apostolate, and the Society of Saint Vincent de Paul, which
is devoted to assisting the needy.

Common to these associations are some fixed prayers that the members are to offer every day, efforts
to imitate the virtues of the saint who is the patron
of the society, and general preparedness to follow
Christ more faithfully. Members are often ready to
make such sacrifices as daily Mass, fasting, almsgiving, Eucharistic adoration, and sometimes even all-
night vigils.

The parish should develop a positive approach to
these popular devotional groups. The Second Vatican Council says that "popular devotions of the
Christian people are to be highly commended, provided they accord with the laws and norms of the
Church. . . . These devotions should be so drawn
up that they harmonize with the liturgical seasons,
accord with the sacred liturgy, are in some fashion
derived from it, and lead the people to it, since, in
fact, the liturgy by its very nature far surpasses any of
them" (*Sacrosanctum Concilium*, 13). The parish priest
can help these associations by visiting them as often
as his schedule allows, by delivering well-prepared
allocutions to them, by getting other priests to help,
and by looking into their prayers to make sure that
they are approved by the bishop. Where the leaders

SPECIAL PARISH APOSTOLATES   135

of some of these associations make undue demands on the members, the priest will find a prudent way to make a necessary correction. In 2002, the Congregation for Divine Worship and the Discipline of the Sacraments issued a 299-page Directory on Popular Piety and the Liturgy. A parish priest will find much encouragement and many suggestions in it.

The members of these devotional organizations generally demonstrate a more than common level of generosity in their Christian lives. They are ready, for instance, to visit the sick or the old, do the needed cleaning of the home, and deliver necessary messages for the bedridden. They are ready and willing to join in the work of charity or solidarity as undertaken by the parish. Some are even ready to be of assistance at the wedding or funeral of the poor. The parish should treasure such readiness and channel it fruitfully.

Individual apostolates also have their importance. The parish will encourage them, without detracting from the role of organized apostolates. As we come near the end of this book, we need to reflect on this dimension.

The Second Vatican Council appreciates the role of the apostolate carried out by a person as an individual. "The individual apostolate, flowing generously from its source in a truly Christian life (cf. Jn 4:14), is the origin and condition of the whole lay apostolate, even of the organized type, and it admits of no substitute. Regardless of status, all laypersons (including those who have no opportunity or possibility for collaboration in associations) are called to this type of apostolate and obliged to engage in it. This type of apostolate is useful at all times and places, but in certain circumstances it is the only one appropriate and feasible" (*Apostolicam Actuositatem*, 16). Indeed, the exercise of the apostolate by the individual will make the spread of the Gospel more extensive and incisive, "because in sharing fully in the unique conditions of the life, work, difficulties and hopes of their sisters and brothers, the lay faithful will be able to reach the hearts of their neighbors, friends, and colleagues, opening them to a full sense of human existence, that is, to communion with God and with all people" (*Christifideles Laici*, 28).

Every Christian should give witness to Christ as an individual parent, doctor, lawyer, teacher, business owner or partner, nurse, taxi driver, pilot, or politician. There are occasions when the indicated way of witnessing to Christ is by individual action. Such occasions occur, for example, when one meets a fellow passenger on an eight-hour flight or in meetings with a companion in the workplace or as a visitor, a client, an employer, a friend, an opponent, or a challenger.

Some people are hesitant when they feel that the person seeking contact with them is sent by a group or is a member of a pressure association. They are more relaxed when they see that what they are involved in is just a person-to-person contact. Moreover, there are situations when an organized apostolate is difficult, forbidden, or suspect, for example, under communistic or dictatorial regimes or in times of religious persecution.

What could be regarded as overemphasis on communal witnessing or organization can at times hide differing individual choices or discourage some fine gifts that some individuals have. It can also forget or marginalize groups like women, the poor, social or ethnic minorities, servants, or the unemployed or make the needs of these groups less visible or hidden below the surface. Organizations tend to make the stronger and more vocal people more visible than the weaker ones. It is important that group approaches and group identity do not drown individual differences or styles or, worse still, kill them. This is one reason why the individual apostolate has no substitute.

Even on the parish level, an exaggerated emphasis on a communal or particularly organized method may offer a dictatorial parish leader a formula to suppress or discourage individual thinking and perpetuate what he regards as the traditional approach. Such a policy could disenfranchise fresh ideas and approaches. Over-conformity can be an enemy of progress or of a fresh ventilation of methods. Enlightened fresh thinkers could then be treated as proud or dangerous innovators who are rocking the boat. If such individuals totally submit, the parish may lose some of the gifts they have brought. A parish should not be afraid of individual apostolates.

These reflections should not be interpreted to mean a discouragement of organized apostolates in the parish or, of course, in the diocese and beyond. There are many challenges, problems, and situations where an organized apostolate at the indicated level is the only answer. It is enough to think of organized forces militating against marriage and the family, of associations that promote abortion and euthanasia, and of social problems that give rise to street children or massive youth unemployment. "It can be helpful for you", Pope Benedict XVI told the lay faithful in Africa, "to form associations in order to continue shaping your Christian conscience and supporting one another in the struggle for justice and peace" (*Africae Munus*, 131).

The task before the parish priest is, therefore, on the one hand, to organize the parish apostolate so that the parish will be a dynamic, evangelizing community and, on the other hand, to explain to his people the necessity of individual apostolates and to encourage and motivate them to undertake such apostolates in their many forms. Both dimensions remain important in order for the parish to be a convincing evangelizer.

～

Conclusion

The demands on the parish priest are serious if the hopes of a parish being an evangelizing one are to be realized. This is going to be the closing reflection. It is clear that no matter how many actors there are in the parish, it is the parish priest who is the leader. Much depends on him, his qualities, and his performance.

To begin with, the parish priest must be a man of prayer. He needs to spend a considerable amount of time each day before Our Lord in the Most Blessed Sacrament, put his plans before the Lord, and ask for his directives and blessing. The Holy Eucharist has to be at the center of his spiritual life and of his apostolate. His Eucharistic devotion will be supported by daily meditative reading of the Sacred Scripture. He needs to be familiar with the *Catechism of the Catholic Church* as well as various papal documents and directives from the diocesan bishop, and he needs to have developed a reading culture focused on serious books.

No doubt, newspapers, the radio, and the television do have their contribution to make to keep the priest informed on the realities of the daily life of his people. And no parish priest can afford to ignore the role of the cell phone in the world of today. But it is also expected that the priest will know when to switch these media off and focus attention on more demanding matters.

The priest needs a tidy desk, an orderly filing system, and at least a minimum selection of books on the faith, pastoral questions, and the Church in general. He will have to ask himself how many hours he should give each day to preparing the homily for the following Sunday, writing an exhortation for the parish bulletin, working on a book or booklet that he is authoring, or reading a serious book.

We all agree that the priest has to travel. But opinions can be divided as to whether he should attend all those events that eat up his time, or as to what his criteria should be for deciding which invitation to accept and which to decline. He needs to ask himself how easy it is for his people to have access to him, even outside his scheduled office hours. Each priest should examine his schedule for the day and seek to find times and places when he will be available.

Where a diocese can arrange a seminar for young parish priests, this will be found very useful. And even more experienced parish priests will benefit from an occasional seminar for all parish priests, since no one fulfills all the requirements of his position once and for all, considering that new developments are to be expected in every service, and moreover that each priest can make progress.

It is true that the parish priest is not the parish. But it is also true that much depends on the type of priest that he is and on his leadership. This is the place to thank all our parish priests and their assistant priests and to wish them God's abundant blessing as they sacrifice themselves to serve parishes that are truly evangelizing ones.

The parish is a gift of the Spirit of the Lord for evangelization at the basic level. So far, no easy replacement for it has been recognized. May the Holy Spirit fill all parishes with his grace so that, full of evangelizing fire, they may all inspire.

~

Papal and Council Documents Cited

Francis, Pope

Address to Italian Catholic Action, Saint Peter's Square, April 30, 2017.

Angelus Message, Saint Peter's Square, March 5, 2017.

Evangelii Gaudium, Apostolic Exhortation on the Proclamation of the Gospel in Today's World, November 24, 2013.

Benedict XVI, Pope

Africae Munus, Post-Synodal Apostolic Exhortation on the Church in Africa in Service to Reconciliation, Justice and Peace, November 19, 2011.

Sacramentum Caritatis, Post-Synodal Apostolic Exhortation on The Eucharist as the Source and Summit of the Church's Life and Mission, February 22, 2007.

Verbum Domini, Post-Synodal Apostolic Exhortation on the Word of God in the Life and Mission of the Church, September 30, 2010.

John Paul II, Pope Saint

Address to the Assembly of CELAM, Port-au-Prince, Haiti, March 9, 1983.

Christifideles Laici, Post-Synodal Apostolic Exhortation on the Vocation and the Mission of the Lay Faithful in the Church and in the World, December 30, 1988.

Ecclesia in Africa, Post-Synodal Apostolic Exhortation on the Church in Africa and Its Evangelizing Mission towards the Year 2000, September 14, 1995.

Ecclesia in America, Post-Synodal Apostolic Exhortation on the Encounter with the Living Jesus Christ: The Way to Conversion, Communion and Solidarity in America, January 22, 1999.

Ecclesia in Asia, Post-Synodal Apostolic Exhortation on Jesus Christ the Savior and His Mission of Love and Service in Asia: ". . . That They May Have Life, and Have It Abundantly" (Jn 10:10), November 6, 1999.

Ecclesia in Europa, Post-Synodal Apostolic Exhortation on Jesus Christ Alive in His Church: The Source of Hope for Europe, June 28, 2003.

Ecclesia in Oceania, Post-Synodal Apostolic Exhortation on Jesus Christ and the Peoples of Oceania:

Walking His Way, Telling His Truth, Living His Life, November 22, 2001.

Fidei Depositum, Apostolic Constitution on the Publication of the Catechism of the Catholic Church Prepared Following the Second Vatican Ecumenical Council, October 11, 1992.

Homily at Holy Mass, Shrine of the Holy Cross, Mogila, Poland, June 9, 1979.

Laetamur Magnopere, Apostolic Letter, in Which the Latin Typical Edition of the Catechism of the Catholic Church Is Approved and Promulgated, August 15, 1997.

Message to Youth, IX and X World Youth Day, November 21, 1993.

Pastores Dabo Vobis, Post-Synodal Apostolic Exhortation on the Formation of Priests in the Circumstances of the Present Day, March 25, 1992.

Pastores Gregis, Post-Synodal Apostolic Exhortation on the Bishop, Servant of the Gospel of Jesus Christ for the Hope of the World, October 16, 2003.

Redemptoris Missio, Encyclical on the Permanent Validity of the Church's Missionary Mandate, December 7, 1990.

Salvifici Doloris, Apostolic Letter on the Christian Meaning of Human Suffering, February 11, 1984.

Paul VI, Pope

Discourse to the Roman Clergy, June 24, 1963.

Evangelii Nuntiandi, Apostolic Exhortation on Evangelization in the Modern World, December 8, 1975.

Second Vatican Council

Apostolicam Actuositatem, Decree on the Apostolate of the Laity, November 18, 1965.

Christus Dominus, Decree concerning the Pastoral Office of Bishops in the Church, October 18, 1965.

Dei Verbum, Dogmatic Constitution on Divine Revelation, November 18, 1965.

Gaudium et Spes, Pastoral Constitution on the Church in the Modern World, December 7, 1965.

Gravissimum Educationis, Declaration on Christian Education, October 28, 1965.

Lumen Gentium, Dogmatic Constitution on the Church, November 21, 1964.

Nostra Aetate, Declaration on the Relation of the Church to Non-Christian Religions, October 28, 1965.

Presbyterorum Ordinis, Decree on the Ministry and Life of Priests, December 7, 1965.

Sacrosanctum Concilium, Constitution on the Sacred Liturgy, December 4, 1963.

Unitatis Redintegratio, Decree on Ecumenism, November 21, 1964.